Tomorrow's Pulpit

The Edwin Stephen Griffith Memorial Lectures were inaugurated in 1970 in memory of Edwin Stephen Griffith, a son of Wales, who in his younger days had hoped to enter the Baptist ministry. After his death, and as a result of his will, the Edwin Stephen and Margaret R. Griffith Trust was created for the benefit of Cardiff Baptist College, Wales, and the National Eisteddfod. It is under this trust that these lectures on preaching were delivered at Cardiff Baptist College, June 12-13, 1973.

Tomorrow's Pulpit

ALEC GILMORE

Lutterworth Press
Guildford and London

TOMORROW'S PULPIT

ISBN 0 7188 2219 6

Printed in the U.S.A. by Judson Press, Valley Forge, PA 19481

CONTENTS

PREFACE

The invitation to deliver the Edwin Stephen Griffith Memorial Lectures in Cardiff Baptist College in the summer of 1973 afforded me an opportunity to examine critically some of the experimental work we had been doing in the church of which I am minister at West Worthing in England. The presence of missionaries returning from the field, the winds of change, and the challenging thoughtfulness of a younger generation all combined to put question marks against our traditional patterns of worship and preaching. It was not difficult to find alternatives and this is what we did. But we knew there would come a point where somebody had to sit down and assess what had been done, its strength and its weakness, as well as the presuppositions that lay behind it. The preparation of these lectures gave me just this opportunity, and in discharging it, I began to see the future just a little more clearly.

While the basic pattern of the book follows that of the New Testament, saying that man is lost, God is present both to teach and to heal, and his death gives man hope, the material which is used in each section to illustrate the points may appear to some to be rather a diverse, not to say motley, collection. To some extent this is true. In part it is material that happens to have come to hand in the last few years; were this book being written in five years time, it would doubtless contain quite different resource material. In part it is material that happens to appeal to those of us who worship each Sunday at West Worthing; were this book being written during a ministry in Birmingham or Manchester (U.K. or U.S.A.), it would have had quite different contents. In part it is random material, for life must be taken at random, and the preacher must relate the gospel to life as it comes and not try to restrict life to some preaching scheme of his own devising. I say this by way of explanation and not apology, for it is an essential tenet of all that follows that the church and the preacher must have such a clear conception of the basics of the gospel that they can literally take anything that appeals to them and anything that life throws at them and relate these things to their faith.

In this respect I was much encouraged in the line I was taking by the appearance of J. G. Davies's *Every Day God*,[1] in which he writes about encountering the holy in word and worship. If any reader wishes to follow the lines proposed here and to find material on a much wider basis than I have indicated, he will find Davies's book a mine of information. Another book which seems to me to be saying similar things from a different angle is Michael H. Taylor's *Variations on a Theme*,[2] in which the principal of Northern Baptist College suggests guidelines for Christians who want to reform the liturgy. The destination is certainly very similar, though he comes at it from the point of view of the liturgy whereas my approach has been based on the life and ministry of Jesus.

In the selection of material and in its interpretation my debts are to many. Where I am aware of my sources, I have always tried to acknowledge them, but ideas have legs, and the preacher collects his ideas in all sorts of strange places. In various ways he either passes them on believing them to be his own, or he subconsciously adapts them and so places his own stamp on them as he goes along. In both cases I wish to record my gratitude.

Finally, I wish to thank the principal of Cardiff Baptist College, the Reverend Dafydd G. Davies, the faculty, and all those who attended the lectures, for the invitation in the first place, for the stimulation of the discussion, and for the warmth of their friendship and hospitality; the Reverend Frank T. Hoadley of Judson Press for his friendship over many years and for being kind enough, when he saw the prospectus, to suggest that the lectures might be published, as well as to his colleague, the Reverend Harold Twiss for seeing the book safely through the press; the members of my own church at West Worthing, whose patience and loyalty have enabled so much to be accomplished and whose wealth of Christian experience has contributed to it; and to one member of that church, Mrs. Julie M. Appleton, for her skillful help in preparing the manuscript.

Alec Gilmore

West Worthing
1974

INTRODUCTION

If there is one aspect of church life that is shared by most Protestants, it is the pulpit. While each denomination has certain traditions that it cherishes, the preaching of the Word has been central in the worship experience. This characteristic has been particularly true of the nonliturgical churches. Congregations have prided themselves on having a minister who enjoys great repute in the community. Ministers are often judged on the quality of their pulpit performances. The Protestant heroes have often been great preachers—Charles Haddon Spurgeon, Dwight L. Moody, and Henry Ward Beecher.

The pulpits are still there, all of them. The preachers are not. Perhaps they never were and it is just distance that lends enchantment to the view. But certainly large conferences and gatherings come and go without any great preacher of notable utterance. Even Billy Graham has been something of an enigma to some of his fans (not to mention his critics!), for they could not understand how one whose preaching was so dull could elicit such response, and many comments made by lay people about us as preachers lead me to believe that at worst we are dull, at best we are competent, but only rarely are any of us captivating.

But then the man in the pew has lost interest in preaching. Sixty minutes has become twenty. The great preaching occasions have been reduced to the level of discussion. People have been told that they must go to church to worship, and not to "hear a preacher." And the minister who was popular has too often been the one who could crowd his diary with engagements, stroke the men, titillate the ladies, and join in horseplay with the young people. Or so it has often appeared, and the appearance has been strong enough to tempt many men to neglect their preaching. Yet I am firmly convinced that there is no single factor more calculated to enable a minister to ride the ups and downs of his ministry without being "thrown" than his ability to lead the worship and to preach effectively, for this is the one thing that affects every member (and not just a group). If a man can pass muster here, he will be forgiven nearly everything else.

Be that as it may, the smaller congregations mean less scope for the preacher's gifts, and few sights are funnier than that of the would-be orator brandishing himself in front of eighteen people as if he were in a Methodist Central Hall before two thousand.

What is more serious for the preacher is that we live in a world which has lost interest in the spoken word and certainly in the monologue. The loss of preachers and their congregations is matched only by the loss of politicians and their audiences. In colleges, and now even in universities, the formal lecture is on the way out. "Even if the lecturer can concentrate for fifty minutes," said a lecturer in a school of architecture to me, "the students certainly can't." Gone is the day when crowds of people flocked to church to hear Mr. So-and-So because he was the one person in the district who was educated and therefore whose opinions and convictions were worth having. Possibly today nearly half his congregation is as well educated as he—and the other half may well be better educated.

While it is not part of my purpose to embark on an analysis of what has happened to the sermon and why the pulpit today is in question, I want, nevertheless, to pick out three factors which for me are significant.

First, *changes have taken place in the education of young children*. These changes have led children to question and not simply to believe what they are told. Furthermore, they have led all of us to put the emphasis on what we SEE and DO rather than on what we hear. To this extent communication has been helping people to find the thimble rather than telling everybody where the thimble is. Or, to put the matter differently, the approach has been to bring education in general into line with mathematical education, for when you teach mathematics, you teach people how to do sums; you don't teach them what the answers are. All this has inevitably had effects on preachers and preaching and has led to the now familiar gibe that the preacher must learn to meet his congregation and can no longer be content to stand in a pulpit six feet above contradiction.

Secondly, *contemporary psychology has led us to put an emphasis on FEELING and REALITY rather than on WORDS*. That is, it is one thing to say you believe something, and it is another thing really to believe it. It is one thing, for example, to get a mother to say, "I love my child"; it is another thing really to bring her to love, heart as well as mind. But unless she loves with her heart as well as her mind, it won't mean much the next time the child is naughty. Similarly, if you make the rewards and punishments high enough and the social pressures strong enough, it is relatively easy to bring a child to share his candy. But that doesn't mean you have made him unselfish. You can only discover that by noticing what he does with his candy when nobody is watching.

What we are really concerned with then is not the achievement of certain patterns of behavior, which could be achieved on the old understanding of preaching where you conveyed the right information by means of words and ideas and then set out in simple form the rewards and punishments, but rather the creation of certain attitudes. We have come to see that straight talking and propaganda are not the only ways (and possibly never the best ways) of bringing about this goal.

Nor must we be misled by the fact that some preachers who are still concerned to be dogmatically orthodox succeed in drawing some of the largest crowds. This may mean simply that there is a ready audience for such preachers among those who believe just what they believe and who wish to be confirmed both in their beliefs and their prejudices. How far preaching of this kind affects those who don't share the beliefs, and how far it builds up a resistance in those who don't want to share them, has yet to be investigated; but we do know that if anything happens to dislodge either preacher or congregation from his fixed position, it can have serious consequences. It is also worth remarking that the alternative to preaching dogmatic certainty is not necessarily the sharing of doubts. It could be the sharing of insights. As Trevor Beason says:

One of the most striking features of the ministry of Jesus, as it is portrayed by the gospel writers, is the extreme care he took to leave his friends and acquaintances free to accept or reject the particular insights which he desired to share with them.[1]

Thirdly, *the advent of television has had a number of side effects,* one of which is that people expect to see something when they are listening. Another is that people get used to a variety of voices and approaches. Nothing stays on the screen for more than a few minutes, if that long; yet many preachers continue with their twenty-minute monologues as if people were still accustomed to nineteenth-century oratory.

Moreover, even if Marshall McLuhan[2] is only half right, it is still true that viewers look for and expect some participation and involvement. Television, according to McLuhan, is a cool medium, or a medium of low definition—more like a cartoon than a logical argument, so leaving the viewer to complete the story for himself and determine what it means. Radio and literature, on the other hand, are hot media or media of high definition. As such they are excellent for conveying facts and arguments but not so good at producing attitudes and reactions. A further clarification of the distinction between hot and cool media is that hot media are directed at only one of the senses (sight or sound, for example) whereas a cool medium is directed at more than one sense and so involves more of the person.

For example, it has been shown that when children watch television, they keep their eyes on the faces of the actors. Even during scenes of physical violence they watch the *facial reactions* rather than the *eruptive action.* Guns, knives, and fists are all bypassed in preference for the facial reaction, so that what makes impact is not so much what people say and do, but what they feel, and this leads McLuhan to describe television not so much as an action, but rather as a re-action, medium.[3]

The effect has been to make us feel part of the action, and some medical students who watched an operation on close-circuit television said afterwards that "they seemed not to be watching an operation, but performing it. They felt that they were holding the scalpel."[4]

Reflections of this involvement of the viewer are to be found in much contemporary theater. The old idea of a stage completely divorced from the audience, with a huge, heavy curtain that opened to let the viewers in on another world, has been giving place to theater in the round, with a set that confronts you as soon as you take your seat and with actors and actresses coming up out of the body of the theater. In its extreme form you no longer go to see a play; you go to be part of a play.

Much of this should not be new to the churchgoer, for the act of worship has long been thought of as a drama. It is a drama in which minister and congregation together are the actors, and part of successful and meaningful worship is knowing your part and being able to play it to the full. But hitherto we have not normally extended this to the idea of preaching, which is still bedeviled by the "us and them" mentality. Small wonder then that in an age when people are looking for involvement, the tradition of preaching does not receive very high marks. Some way must be found to maintain a proper emphasis on preaching without necessarily restricting it to a sermon or monologue, and at the same time using what we know of communication in other spheres to help us, as preachers and churches, to proclaim our message, bearing in mind always that what dictates the method of communication is not the subject to be communicated but the audience to whom the communication is made.

If we now bring together these three factors, we begin to see that current patterns of education have led people to question; contemporary psychology has led to a fresh emphasis on feelings and experience; and the television medium has produced a generation that is used to being involved with the whole of being. We must now go on to ask what significance these factors have for the future of the pulpit.

At the risk of a slight exaggeration the picture just presented tends to produce one of two reactions. Either it leads one to say that the day of preaching therefore is done or it leads one to say that whatever happens in the world around us, preaching is always vital and we must go on doing it. Neither reaction is very helpful, for the one is too sweeping and the other too stubborn. It would be better to ask the question: What is preaching?

Thirty years ago it was fashionable in some circles to seek the answer to that question by reference to C. H. Dodd's *The Apostolic Preaching and Its Developments*.[5] One of Dodd's great points in that book was the distinction between preaching *(kerygma)* and teaching *(didaskein)*. I have never been sure that it is a distinction that is as sharp as Dodd made out, but I don't have any doubts when Dodd goes on to stress that in the New Testament *kerygma* is proclamation. "A *keryx* [for example,] may be a town crier, an auctioneer, a herald, or anyone who lifts up his voice and claims public attention for some definite thing he has to announce." [6] Normally, Dodd continues, the verb "to preach" has "the gospel" for its object, so much so that the Greek *keryssein* is almost synonymous with *evangelizesthai* (i.e., to proclaim nearly always means to proclaim the good news about Jesus Christ). [7] If we are to come to grips with what we are to understand by preaching, it is much better to begin here than to begin with preaching as it was handed on to us a decade or so ago or even with preaching as it was known in the Welsh valleys at the turn of the century or in the great days of Sankey and Moody.

From this simple definition Dodd then goes on to work out the character and content of the early preaching by studying Paul and the other early missionary preachers, and this leads him to the conclusion that "The Pauline *kerygma*, therefore, is a proclamation of the facts of the death and resurrection of Christ in an eschatological setting which gives significance to the facts." [8] This definition has been interpreted by some preachers to mean that true preaching is the proclamation of the facts of the death and resurrection of Christ. If for the moment we forget the eschatological setting, it is not difficult to find evidence in the Acts of the Apostles that this is what the early preachers did. They told the story, and it is not uncommon to point out that the one occasion when Paul deviated from this pattern (at Athens) goes down in history as one of his less successful moments as a preacher.

Put like that, it is not difficult to point out a contrast between the preaching of Paul and the apostles on the one hand and the preaching of Jesus on the other. With Jesus the act of proclamation was not so much a matter of words but rather a matter of action. With the early church it was not so much a matter of action but rather a matter of words. Jesus actually brought the goodness with him in his own person and in his involvement with people. The early church repeated the story and talked about it.

The distinction admittedly is not a final one. It is true that Jesus did both talk and teach, but even his words were words that embodied action and led to action. They had about them the quality of many of the prophets of the Old Testament, and, as with

God himself, he spoke and it was done. They were not words that simply reported something that had happened somewhere else. It actually happened where Jesus was, whether he spoke or took action.

Equally, it is true that this sometimes happened when the apostles were around, and we have the story of the lame man healed by Peter and John as they went into the temple; yet increasingly it is clear that, as the story moves on, the preachers tended to settle for words that looked back rather than for action that looked forward. Preaching *in* and *by means of* response thus degenerates into preaching *for* response, and all too soon the response is a vocal affirmation or acceptance of the truth of the words spoken. We are invited simply to believe that what the preacher says is true and to model our lives accordingly.

What we have lost sight of in the preaching of the early church, and in Dodd's definition of it, is the eschatological setting. We have used our preaching to invite people to respond to something that happened at a different time and in a different place, whereas if only we had kept closer to the spirit of Jesus and the incarnation, we would have been using our preaching to produce (not invite, but actually produce!) a response *in* the here and now *to* the here and now. For Jesus, incarnation, redemption, and judgment are not three events that belong to the past, the present, and the future, but three inseparable events that belong to the NOW. This must always be the case if preaching is to be effective.

To clarify what we are saying, we will take just one illustration. Easter Sunday is an opportunity to preach the resurrection. How do we do it? When I was in college, one of our professors told us what he thought was a hair-raising story of an American church on Easter Sunday. On arrival, the visitor found the whole place in darkness as if in mourning. When the service was due to begin, a funeral cortège made its way up the aisle, complete with bier and casket. When it reached the front, the lid shot off; the preacher got up and preached a sermon on the resurrection! Of course it probably never happened. Englishmen love stories like that about Americans, just as Americans love stories about Englishmen who actually walk to work! Neither is it quite what we are advocating, but at least it illustrates some desire that the proclamation shall be more than words.

In more sober fashion, the usual way of preaching the Easter message is by means of a service in which you sing hymns about rolling away the stone and Jesus having conquered death. In the sermon, the preacher will then go on to tell the story and to emphasize the fact that the grave really was empty, Mary and the disciples really did meet him, and Thomas (who had the audacity to doubt) finally had to surrender. From there he may then go on to produce authenticating "proofs" for what, after all, can only be a spiritual experience. If that is not enough, he will proceed to recite the benefits that flow from the resurrection. He will tell you that there is now meaning in suffering (ignoring the question from the little boy on the front row who asks why Jesus doesn't heal the blind lady he knows, as he did in the New Testament) and that because of the resurrection we can face death with hope (ignoring the little girl on the second row whose father died last week and who feels as if she has no hope at all). In conclusion we shall be invited to believe that all that the preacher says is true and that all the benefits of which he speaks will be ours if only we can accept this matter of the resurrection.

In some respects the situation has been overdrawn, but it is not necessarily all that wide of the mark. We shall not pause to examine the validity of such an approach to Easter Sunday, for that is not what we are after. Suffice it to say that it is possible to *believe* with all your heart that Jesus rose from the dead and yet never to enjoy the benefits of that victory, just as it is possible to believe that ocean-going liners get safely to the other side of the Atlantic without yourself ever having the joys of foreign travel.

The question we want to ask is, "How did Jesus proclaim the resurrection?" And the answer is, "By rising." He didn't *tell* anybody anything, and such broad hints as he did drop were either ignored or misunderstood. He didn't ever invite them to do anything or believe anything. He simply behaved in such a way that new life was born. When they were in despair, they found hope. When they came to what they thought was the end, they suddenly discovered it was the beginning. When life seemed pointless, they found a reason for living.

If therefore we are to preach the resurrection today, it will not be sufficient that we invite people to accept something that happened over nineteen hundred years ago. What matters is that we learn to recognize the new life of Christ here and now and enable our people to respond to that.

This line of argument is not to denigrate what the preaching of the early church was about, but rather to give to it a new significance. An appreciation of the preaching of the early church is crucial not in the sense that we must tell the story they told, but rather in the sense that as they pointed to the activity of the risen Lord in their generation, so we must be prepared to point to the activity of the risen Lord in ours. Furthermore, it is in studying the basic characteristics of their experience and their preaching that we are able to discern what to look for and where to point. The preaching of the early church is rather like a guide to a department store—it doesn't list every single item you can find, but it does tell you the main departments worth visiting and invite you to go and rummage for yourself. Over the years the departments will change little, if at all, but the actual wares will change according to culture, climate, fashion, personal taste, and so on.

Similarly with the preaching of the early church—the main framework never varies, but the details do. Circumcision, to take but one example, is no longer very relevant over most of the Western world, but the issues that lie behind the circumcision controversy, such as respect for the past, respect for the opinion of others, or the nature of the Christian community, are as relevant as ever they were. Our criticism of much contemporary preaching is that too many preachers have been more content to pass on the guide to the department store than they have actually to market the wares.

If we may go back now to C. H. Dodd, his book is of value because by picking out the salient features of apostolic preaching, Dodd clearly indicates for us the topics on which our "proclamation happenings" have to be based. Dodd in fact located seven facets to the Good News:[9]

1. The coming of Jesus Christ inaugurates a new age.
   We are now living in it and prophecy is fulfilled. (This is substantially what we have been arguing thus far. We are to find Christ in our present age and he will be relevant neither in the past nor in the future if he is not first seen to be relevant in the present.)
2. Jesus Christ belongs to the line of David.
3. He died to deliver us from this present age.
4. He was buried.
5. He rose again on the third day.

6. He is exalted at the right hand of God.

7. He will come again as judge and savior.

Dodd then goes on further to say that the proclamation of the message always concluded with an appeal for repentance, the offer of forgiveness, and the gift of the Holy Spirit, leading to the establishment of a new community.[10] That is to say, even in the early church the event was a here-and-now event that was related to what had gone before and was more than a simple belief in what had gone before.

Partly because our day is different from that of Paul and the apostles (if only in the sense that it is separated in time by a longer period from the event of Jesus Christ himself), and partly because it is different from the days in which Dodd wrote (for theology never stands still), we will take those same points and give them a slight recast. We begin by asking the question, "If Jesus proclaimed by his life in such a way as actually to bring about a change in people, what in fact did he do?" To that, we find four answers.

1. He became incarnate. He became a man among men, and in so doing he showed up the poverty of human life as he found it. He was like a light shining in a dark place.

2. He told stories in such a way as to create in men an awareness of "another world" while living in this world. It was an awareness of a new dimension, a presence, of himself and therefore of God, a God incarnate. And it was this awareness of God that enabled them to recognize the reality of their own condition as one of lostness or slavery.

3. He performed miracles, and by so doing he either released them from their chains and restrictions or stood by them and shared their trials. But in either case his presence was sufficient to change their lives.

4. By being free himself, by defying slavery, and by refusing to become what people wanted to make of him, even to the point of death, he opened up a new way for the future for himself and for others. His very being had released another power into the world—God—as never before.

Another way of expressing it is in the more familiar words, "he was born, he suffered and died, he rose again and gives the same spirit to others." This is the basic Good News. This is what happened in the Gospels and it is, according to Dodd, what the early preachers proclaimed. It is also what we learn from the three Christian festivals of Christmas, Easter, and Pentecost.

This then is what we must proclaim, remembering that to proclaim it is not simply to say that it happened two thousand years ago, to report it, and relate it, and then to invite people to make a decision about it, but rather to embody all this in life and worship in the here and now in such a way that people are led to make the response of repentance, forgiveness, and acceptance.

To this extent proclamation is life, but since it is a fundamental point that the liturgy of the church embodies the whole of the gospel in itself, it is worth remarking that this discovery of the presence of God and man's unworthiness before him belongs to what we may call the preparation for worship, or the opening gambit. It is the experience such as that of Isaiah in the temple where everything begins:

> In the year that King Uzziah died I saw the Lord sitting upon a throne, high and lifted up; and his train filled the temple. Above him stood the seraphim; each had six wings: with two he covered his face, and with two he covered his feet, and with two he flew. And one called to another and said:
> "Holy, holy, holy is the Lord of hosts;
> the whole earth is full of his glory."
> And the foundations of the thresholds shook at the voice of him who called, and the house was filled with smoke (Isaiah 6:1-4).

When you have an experience like that, in the temple or out of the temple, you may know that God is not very far away.

FINDING THE LOST

As soon as Isaiah became aware of the holy in his life, he suddenly became conscious of his own unworthiness. Like light showing up dust in a dark corner, so Jesus' very presence in the world is one that makes man acutely aware of his lostness. He is out of harmony with himself and with his fellows, and therefore with God.

Jesus doesn't achieve this effect by going around telling people that they are lost, but rather by living and patterning his life in such a way that three things happen:

1. People in his presence *feel* lost. In some cases this is simply because their own lives strike them as impoverished compared with his; in other cases it is because of something he deliberately says or does which raises a question in their minds.

2. Though a person may feel *lost,* he is nevertheless always left with the feeling that when Jesus is around, he is *wanted.* On the part of Jesus this is deliberate and calculated. He goes out of his way to make people feel that they matter to him, and he usually succeeds in helping them to feel that they matter to at least one other person also.

3. Once a person is aware of his condition, he is presented with a *choice.* He may either continue in his isolation or he may respond by opening himself to someone else.

Luke 15 is a good illustration. The first two stories of the lost coin and the lost sheep are simply stories about lostness, doubtless related by Jesus at some point and later added to the more crucial event of the two sons. We use the word "event" advisedly because by the time you get to the end of the story, it is clear that something has happened to the hearers. It is now apparent in fact that this is not a story of a lost son but a tale of two lost sons. Both are lost and estranged from the father, one in a far country and the other in a barricade of self-righteousness and self-justification. But since in the beginning the hearers had no difficulty in identifying characters, and even went the step further of identifying themselves with the elder brother, it is a double blow, when Jesus comes to the end, to discover that he is in fact talking about them. They feel, and they don't like what they feel.

They suddenly realize that they have lost out somewhere, and unlike Nathan, who had to deal with David after the incident with Uriah's wife (2 Samuel 12:1-7), Jesus has no need ever to say, "Thou art the man." They know, and they are angry. In this moment they begin to see themselves, rather than others, as lost, estranged from the Father and from one another, in stark contrast to the freedom and self-confidence of Jesus. It is in moments like this that they are prodded to ask him who he thinks he is; yet he has never claimed to be anyone, not even to pass comments on them. He has not even begun to judge anyone, but they have judged themselves.

At the same time there is sufficient in the story for them to realize that this is not a story Jesus tells in order to reject them. The father in the story goes out of his way to make it clear to the elder brother that he is every bit as much wanted as the second boy, and the relevance of that point will not be lost on the hearers. But even so it is a story without an ending. The element of choice is there, and Jesus does not presume to tell his hearers how the elder brother chose. Did he repent and go in to the banquet or did he stay outside gnashing his teeth? This is for the hearers to determine, for at this point the story has faded into second place and the event is the event of judgment.

Effective preaching therefore is learning to create situations which in themselves may seem quite harmless and inoffensive and which claim nothing for us as preachers but which nevertheless bring home to men and women the real state and condition of their lives. This is preaching judgment, and it is a very different thing from preaching hellfire, which may frighten people into adopting certain desired lines of action but which does not necessarily ever present them with an awareness of how lost they are. It is commonplace today to say that preachers no longer preach judgment. If by that is meant that we don't preach hellfire, then I for one want to say "Thank God," but if by that is meant that we don't order our worship and preaching so that people are made to feel their lostness, then I think "What a tragedy!" Take this element away from Jesus' ministry and you have no starting point, though the preacher who indulges in it may find that he preaches to smaller congregations. Hellfire preaching has certain attractions—the "saved" like to think of others being dangled over the pit. True preaching of judgment has few attractions, and there are sure to be some who cannot stand the heat and who melt away. It happened like that with Jesus.

In order to achieve this quality in preaching, we must first of all be quite clear what we mean when we say that man is lost or a sinner or a slave. It is because many pulpiteers are vague at this point that their message lacks bite.

Suppose we go back to Genesis 1-2 and try to see the story of Adam and Eve as a myth, or a glorious symbol for all time of our human condition. (If the reader wishes to believe in Adam and Eve as historical fact, it will still not invalidate the point we are making.) First of all, you have to rid your mind of any suggestion that somewhere in the narrative God has changed. A superficial reading seems to suggest that he has—that before Adam and Eve were disobedient, he was all smiles and sweetness, good and kind, offering them the earth and telling them to rule over it; whereas after they were disobedient, he turned nasty, drove them out of the garden, and took good care that they didn't come back. But of course God has not changed. What happened is that Adam and Eve came to feel differently about him. Man alienates himself from the one who wants to love him and then concludes that the other Person is a vicious monster who is trying to destroy him. This is what is meant by alienation or sin. It is seeing God as being on the other side and against you.

This feeling of alienation is often then accompanied by a withdrawal from responsibility. Adam blames Eve. Eve blames the serpent, with the result that the God who only a little while before seemed to be actually encouraging them to eat of the Tree of Life now seems to exclude them from the Garden before they get at the Tree of Life. Hitherto, they felt it was God's intention that they should have everything and be in control, whereas now that they are withdrawn, they feel quite different about him.

At this point we can perceive the difference between the Full Life and the Fallen Life. The Full Life is where man is free and open in the Garden—open to God, open to his neighbors, and open to the world. The Fallen Life is the life where man has withdrawn from his fellows and from responsibility; he lives in fear of God and his brethren and feels the need of some sort of protection.

John Wren-Lewis sees this concept reflected in man's nakedness followed by his desire for some sort of clothing. His nakedness is a symbol of his openness. After "the fall" his sudden desire for clothing is a sign of his alienation. Similarly he refers to people who have nude dreams. They are often afraid to share such dreams with their psychologist because they feel their dreams have something to do with sex, but Wren-Lewis alleges that nudity in dreams rarely has anything to do with sex; it is much more related to "vulnerability and unprotectedness."[1] We don't like to think of ourselves as nude because we don't like to think of ourselves as unprotected and open to others.

No doubt we shall go on debating the details of this *schema* for a long time, but there can be no doubt about the broad thesis; and if it is only partially correct, it may well explain further why in an acquisitive society we not only invest in clothes but also in houses and gardens and even garden fences, why the automobile is so much more attractive than public transport, and why we have to have our investments and our insurance policies, whereas societies with fewer possessions seem to have a greater openness toward others.

Perhaps the one tree we must not eat of is the "opting-out tree"— the tree which leads us to avoid the full responsibility in the community and drives us in on ourselves. To eat of it is a perennial temptation, and to succumb to the temptation is to die to life. So it was that the younger boy in Luke 15 isolated himself by collecting his own share and then cutting himself off from the family circle in order to make the most of it. His elder brother no less isolated himself within the family and resolutely refused to accept his responsibility for his brother.

This is our lot and it is the lot of our fellowmen. It is the fruit of sin, lostness, and slavery, and in New Testament terms we are the people of whom it is said, "We piped to you, and you did not dance" (Luke 7:32). Or, to change the reference, we are like people who are invited to a party and who refuse to go. So let us look more closely.

In examining this familiar story (Luke 14:15-24), we find an incident which not only illustrates the nature of our lostness, but shows also the deftness of Jesus in bringing it home to people because it all begins with a man who is lost and doesn't know he's lost. Jesus hears him utter a pious hope, such as the lost often do, "Won't it be wonderful for those people who are able to sit down in heaven with God!" And from the way he said it, he made it pretty clear that he intended to be one of them. But Jesus says, "You know, it's not really going to be like that at all. The kingdom of God is here and now, only the people who ought to see it can't (or won't) see it." They are like people invited to a party who refuse to go.

It is significant that Jesus chose a party. Read the story and you see that these people were all good people, but they were preoccupied with home and family interests to the point where home and family insulated them against everybody else. With one it was his wife, with one it was his work and with one it was his latest "toy." If they had been invited to a family event or to the next meeting of the Camera Club, or if somebody had been in trouble and in need of help, no doubt they would all have rallied to it—but not to a party, because a party is just a place where you meet people and do nothing. We don't mind meeting people—in fact we quite like it if there is some purpose to it—but not for meeting's sake.

In this way Jesus accentuates the point of Genesis 1-2, and he shows how fallen man not only isolates himself from his fellows but also sees them as those with whom he can share a common purpose rather than simply as those whom he can meet. Politicians see people as potential voters; advertisers see people as potential consumers; some men see women as potential sex partners; and preachers see people as potential Christians. Moreover, it's a sobering thought to reflect on the number of times any of us meets a person for the sake of a relationship pure and simple. Far more often we assess people not according to the depth of relationship we can have with them but according to whether they help us to further our aims (in which case we like them) or they hinder our own fulfillment (in which case we don't!).

There may be other reasons why fallen man is not too keen on parties. Perhaps it is because of all events in life the party is the least structured. You know where you are at home. At work you fit into a pattern. Even in a club each person has his place. But at a party it's the same for all, and nobody knows what will happen. This is why parents feel safer when their adolescent offspring go to a club or to evening classes than when they just go to a party.

Our rigidity contrasts so much with the image of Jesus as found in the New Testament, and I think we ought to be grateful to *Godspell* for bringing it home to us. *Godspell* is perhaps more of a pantomime than a party, but the atmosphere is the same. It's a place where people are not preoccupied with themselves or their lives, but are ready simply to engage with one another in the joy of living. When I saw *Godspell*, I remember, I had the feeling that this was just how it all was before we read the New Testament in our churches, wrote weighty commentaries on it, and preached long sermons on it. Originally it was fun and everybody enjoyed it, except those long-faced people who were too lost to laugh. It seemed to make sense, even when they said that Jesus was Ginger Rogers.

If the nature of man's lostness is still not clear to you, contrast the sort of person who just loves a wedding because he has nothing to do but talk to people, which is what he loves, with that other person who would only go to a wedding if he were taking photographs and so would have no need to meet people, which is what he hates. He can hide behind his camera. He is at the party, and yet he is not at the party.

And contrast all those people who were preoccupied with home and work and pleasure with Tarrou in Albert Camus' *The Plague.* Tarrou is the sanitary officer in a French town that is destined to destruction by a plague, and not only does he keep his faith in himself to the extent of carrying on faithfully with his work when all is lost, but also at the height of the plague he actually takes time off to go for a swim "for friendship's sake," because as he says,

Really, it's too damn silly living only in and for the plague. Of course, a man should fight for the victims, but if he ceases caring for anything outside that, what's the use of his fighting?[2]

It's at the party (or the swim) that we begin to see who we are and why we are, and perhaps our unwillingness to attend the party is a fear of facing the truth.

How then do we bring home to contemporary man his lost condition in such a way as to make him feel wanted and to present him with a choice, for it is not sufficient that we find him in his lostness unless we are able also to point him away from his lostness?

Simon and Garfunkel have an album, "The Sounds of Silence," in which there is a song which says something about the words of the prophets being written on subway walls. What the actual words are that are written on the subway walls doesn't matter. The point is that the word of God is writ large in the world. People read, but they don't always hear. Preaching, therefore, in order to help a person become aware of his lostness is not so much angling our message in such a way that he feels lost but rather opening his ears and eyes in such a way that he becomes aware of his lostness in the world around him because of what he sees in that world. Our message is helping him to perceive the depth of the ordinary.

This approach to preaching has two results. First, it enables a man to do his own listening, anywhere and everywhere, and therefore it affords a greater opportunity for God to get through to him. But secondly, when the message hits home, the hearer believes it not because the Reverend Mr. So-and-So says it and therefore it must be true, but because the very truth has stabbed his own heart.

But it won't stab his heart awake unless it has first stabbed the preacher's heart to an appreciation of his own lostness and the lostness of his fellowmen. Therefore, ways of studying together those things that bring the message home need to be found.

One way of doing this is to read or see or listen to (it's available on a record) Edward Albee, *The Zoo Story*.[3] It's a fifty-minute dialogue between two men, each of whom is shut up in himself. The scene is set in New York's Central Park. Jerry sits down on a park bench one Sunday afternoon and starts talking to Peter, who is there. At first Jerry's reception is friendly, but when he encroaches too far, Peter becomes resistant. He makes it clear that it is his bench—he goes there every Sunday afternoon. Peter is happy to answer Jerry's questions, except that every so often you become aware that Jerry is probing too far and Peter shuts up.

Jerry has tried hard to make relationships with people but always without success. He loves the little ladies, but only for an hour—and he has never been able to make love with anyone more than once. He has no relationship with the other people in the same apartment building and has not found it easy to get on with the landlady. In desperation he has tried to get on with the landlady's dog and even that has failed. Peter, on the other hand, is happily married and has two daughters and two parakeets, but he, too, has never quite been able to cope with life. When Jerry becomes threatening, there is an amusing scene in which Peter starts frantically calling for the police and so epitomizes the way of many who in desperation meet a desperate situation by saying that the law—the government—the church should do something!

What is actually said in the play (the story) is less important than what is felt, and that is why the play must be experienced for itself. Unless the congregation is small, it is probably not the thing for a church service, but there are ways in which it can be handled. A preacher, for example, might wrestle with it himself until he has come to grips with the feel of it and actually knows what it *feels* like to be lost. He might even put the play side by side with the story of the two sons in Luke 15 and see what they say to each other. Having done this, he is in a much better position to preach about lostness than he was before.

Another way of dealing with it is to invite a group of ten or a dozen more thoughtful members of the congregation to listen to the play one evening and then to discuss it. Suggest that they try to get inside the characters, to relate them to similar people in the New Testament story and to see what Jesus did with them, and to think of contemporary people in a similar state. By the end of the evening everybody will have felt something fresh about the human predicament. By this stage all of them will not only *know* that man is lost, but also they will *feel* that he is, and they will know, too, what it is to want to be wanted.

In some cases it might even be possible for a group to present the theme in church with a couple of readers and one or two short extracts to enable the play to speak for itself. Quite a lot could be conveyed in five minutes, and if the attempt led a congregation at the beginning of its worship to come to grips with where the gospel begins, it would not only be using the pattern of worship in the way it ought to be used (that is, to recite the faith before God and man) but it would also enrich the experience of the worshipers. The words on the subway walls would begin to shout more loudly.

In some respects this is what the prayer of confession at the beginning of a service is meant to achieve, but how dull and wordy we often are! Why not use a story like this from Solzhenitsyn?

The Bonfire and the Ants

I threw a rotten log onto the fire without noticing that it was alive with ants.
   The log began to crackle, the ants came tumbling out and scurried around in desperation. They ran along the top and writhed as they were scorched by the flames. I gripped the log and rolled it to one side. Many of the ants then managed to escape onto the sand or the pine needles.
   But, strangely enough, they did not run away from the fire.
   They had no sooner overcome their terror than they turned, circled, and some kind of force drew them back to their forsaken homeland. There were many who climbed back onto the burning log, ran about on it, and perished there.[1]

Not much imagination is needed to see the connection between that and our human predicament, and only a sentence or a relevant Scripture passage is needed to drive the point home. If the preacher, however, wanted to tarry a little longer with the contemporary, he could play the song, "Where Have All the Flowers Gone?" which brings out the same point of our human folly. To begin here is to begin where man is.

Once we even begin to bring home to our congregation a sense of lostness, each in turn will start looking for an exit. Similarly, where you find a person who is always looking for a way out, you have at least one sign that that person is lost. So why not take the theme "Looking for Exits" and spend a month collecting material so as to present the theme more fully?

There are simple signs that often point to deeper symptoms. When some people go to the theater or enter any public building, the first thing they do is to look around to see where the exits are. When they go into a hotel room, the first thing they do is to read all the fire precautions, after which they go to locate the emergency staircase. In an airplane they sit by the emergency exit. In church they sit on the back row!

If you are not that sort of person, you may smile at such stupidity, but you may have other symptoms that are not very different. What happens when you know you have broken the law with your car? You exceeded the speed limit on the highway and didn't know what you were doing until you saw the end of the limit sign. Then you see a car that could be a highway patrol—do you immediately try to convince yourself that it isn't the police and yet start thinking up reasons, excuses, and defenses? Because if you do, you are looking for exits, too. And, like the man in church when we begin to confront him with his lostness, we never look more frantically than when we think our sense of lostness is about to be brought to the surface.

In the Bible, Jeremiah is a good example:

> O that I had in the desert
> a wayfarers' lodging place,
> that I might leave my people
> and go away from them!
> (Jeremiah 9:2)

There are also parallels in the life of Jesus that reward study. Jeremiah goes through spells when he wishes he had never been born, and when (having been born) he wishes he had never been burdened with the kind of life he's got. There is no sorrow like his sorrow, and he begins to be aware of the price he will have to pay if no way out presents itself.

When he clearly sees that the door is closed to him, there is an interesting turn of events, and you begin to see what happens to a man who is lost when all exits are cut off. Jeremiah hopes and prays for vengeance on his enemies. If there is to be no way out for him, at least he can drag down a few others with him.

It is here then that you begin to see the contrast between Jeremiah and Jesus—the one who is lost and who therefore opts out of all relationships and the one who is God and who therefore is able to take other people's burdens on himself. The lost man will wear out his knuckles battering on the closed door; God simply accepts the fact willingly that the door is shut. Jesus now knows his fate. He will grasp the nettle. He will pull down the storm clouds over himself.

In this way Jesus demonstrates for all time that once we are able to accept the situation from which there is no exit, we receive new sources of power with which to go forward. And he doesn't only *demonstrate,* as if to say, "Go and do thou likewise," but by his action he releases the power which makes it possible for others to live without exits, too.

Once these principles are clear and this biblical framework is appreciated, then it should be possible to collect material from the contemporary situation—extracts from plays, poetry, songs, experiences, and newspaper cuttings. The preacher who can then present the contemporary in the light of the fundamental will have no difficulty in leading his congregation to an awareness of what the Bible understands by man's lostness.

When we handled this theme, one of the current items of news was a new film called *Family Life* in which the star was Jan, an attractive, weak but willful working-class girl who never got on with her parents, who were kindly and caring but who never knew quite what to do. Jan was nearly driven mad as she tried to be true to herself and to live her own life in what was largely an alien and unsympathetic environment. At one point her anger was such that she and her boyfriend sprayed the garden with washable paint. On another occasion she smashed her father's treasured clock, all of which sounds grim, but deep down it was all because Jan sensed that there was something far better to life than she had yet discovered and she was looking for an exit from her misery to a richer life. She knew this, though she could not formulate it or deal with it. She knew she was lost. When this story is put in the setting just outlined, it tells you something about what the Bible means and it also tells you something about Jan's state.

Doubtless Jan is an extreme case, but she is only an extreme case of a typical condition—an extreme case of any woman trying to escape from the kitchen sink or any man trying to find a more satisfying job.

In all this, however, we are still at the level of talk and thought. Somehow we have to become absorbed in our thought to such an extent that we actually create the atmosphere that Jesus created. We have to create the "party atmosphere" where people feel it for themselves so that talking becomes superfluous. This, ideally, must be what brings home to a man his sense of lostness and the fact that he is needed. How do we do it? Perhaps it has something to do with the way we think of our churches.

Not long ago a clergyman went into a bookstore and picked up a book of prayers. Turning to the back, he found "Dreams for Celebration" where he read, "Someday soon people will send up balloons in church/Turn tired old cathedrals into cafeterias." [5] He took it literally and it offended him. But when he got home, he reflected on it and did his own dream. Now he is sold on the book, and this simple story set me dreaming, too.

We all know not only what a cathedral looks like but what it feels like as well. You have only to look at a picture. It's large, solid, unchanging, and unadaptable. Go inside and you have your

history and your ancestors around your ears. The very age of the
building makes you feel rather like the two-year-old gazing for the
first time at his great-grandmother; surely she must have been there
since the world began!

There's a coldness and an aloofness about the place, too. The
high, vaulted roof may give you a vision of heaven, but at the same
time it seems to tell you that you'll never get up there. The organ
music thunders out from nowhere like the voice of God on Sinai.
The preacher stands in his ivory tower and offers you the words of
life, but you'll be lucky if you ever shake his hand. What is offered
is a deposit of truth. It is rooted in the past and is still there in the
present. It will never come to you, but you can come and collect
what is offered if you wish.

But the cafeteria is quite different. I pop in at the railway station
for a quick cup of coffee, and as soon as I go in through the door, I
feel the warmth. There are no distinctions between the people—the
man who is well dressed may choose not to come in; but if he does
come in, he's the same as everybody else. There is no real
distinction between those who serve and those who are served.
They may wear different clothes and stand on opposite sides of the
counter, but at least you feel as if you all belong to the same society.

What is offered here is each according to his need. There is
something for the person who wants a quick bite to hold him until
he gets home; there is a balanced diet for the person who has to eat
there every day; and there is a full service for those who may depend
on it for their main meal of the day for a short period of their lives
before moving on to other pastures.

In one case you have the atmosphere of the law courts; in the
other case you have the atmosphere of the party. Both have their
places in society. But when you read the New Testament, there is
no doubt where Jesus was most at home, nor is there any doubt
where men and women became aware of their real state and found
hope. If the message is to get through in our churches, it may be
that we have to look at the way we create atmosphere in our
churches before we ever stop to think what is actually said there.
Jim Bates's prayer, "Praise God for Coffee Bars," has got
something of the same point.[6]

There are many routes which lead a person to a sense of lostness
that leads to hope, and we have looked only at one or two of them,
but at least we have begun to sense the experience many a person

had when he or she got near to Jesus. The good church, the good pastor, the good preacher, and the good pattern of worship should have just the same effect.

This, too, belongs to the opening act of worship or preparation for worship, and as such follows the initial impression of awe and holiness. This is how it happened with Isaiah:

And I said: "Woe is me! For I am lost; for I am a man of unclean lips, and I dwell in the midst of a people of unclean lips; for my eyes have seen the King, the Lord of hosts!" (Isaiah 6:5)

ESTABLISHING
A
PRESENCE

When Paul was struck with physical blindness on the road to Damascus, and so came to a real awareness of his spiritual state, he says that the first question he asked was, "Who are you, Lord?" And when he received the answer that it was Jesus, his second question was, "What shall I do, Lord?" (See Acts 22:1-10.) It is the natural reaction of a lost man. He wants a reassurance that the power that has brought him this far can take him further, and so he must learn to recognize that power and to be able to identify with it.

This is what we mean by establishing a presence or (to be more precise) the awareness of a presence. In theological terms it is a realization of the incarnation, the discovery that you can find God in flesh, and therefore in the flesh that is around you, provided you realize that it is of the very nature of the incarnate God that he cannot be tied down. Paul could not guarantee that God would meet him again on the Damascus Road or that God would meet anybody else there who was going through a similar experience. He could not even guarantee to others that God had ever been there at all. So it always is with the presence of God. You may say, "Lo, here!" or "Lo, there!" but you can never even hope that other people will agree with you.

Try to see this truth first in relationship to Moses. You and I may have no doubt that Moses was a godly presence, a man in whom God was constantly at work, but it can't have escaped your notice that not everybody sees him that way, and in his lifetime there were very many who did not see him that way at all. He may have been something of a divine leader to the children of Israel (or to *some* of the children of Israel), but he was something very different to the Egyptians. He may have been god to Aaron, but he was the very devil to Pharaoh.

All this goes to show that you can't point anywhere or to any person and say unequivocally, "That's God!" or "That is the work of the Holy Spirit!" And the preacher who does make such claims must be prepared for two reactions: first, not everybody will agree with him; and, second, some people will actually call good what he calls evil and vice versa. Preaching is by no means a certain art calling forth a single response.

In the case of Moses it was not only Pharaoh and the Egyptians who rejected him as a man in whom God worked. Many of his own people refused to recognize him; so when he had tried hard to get through with his message and failed, he did the only thing he could do. He took no notice of what they said but simply and quietly carried on among his people. His presence established their confidence until they were prepared to recognize his authority; for until that happened, nothing else could. Then, all at once, and this time without any great rhyme or reason, Moses said, "Come on— we're going," and they went. The presence had established itself through trust. (It was not only the presence and the trust, as we see in chapter 3; it was also the element of miracle. But it was the trust that enabled the miracle to be given a meaningful interpretation.)

Something very similar happened in the case of Jesus. His authority, like that of Moses, was not only challenged by his enemies but also was often misunderstood by his friends. They didn't always see what he was driving at. They didn't always agree with him when they did. Support was always unevenly spread even among those who were nearest to him—Thomas was obviously doubting the whole thing to the very end; and they didn't all recognize Jesus in the same way even on the resurrection morning—but over a period of three years he gradually established his leadership and authority among a handful. Even the crowds came to recognize that nobody had spoken like this before, and after three years men who at the start had no idea what they were taking on grew to the point where they would do almost anything for him. If they failed him at the last, it was only because they felt that once he was captured the game was up and they just couldn't go on alone. Three days later, their conviction about the resurrection was only possible because of the ultimate authority which they had granted to him.

The moral of all this for the preacher may well be that he, too, has to learn to win his authority slowly among his congregation, but this is not the point we wish to make. The significant thing for our purpose now is that the response to God's word will always be uneven and confused. The presence of God is not something we can establish as we might establish a scientific or mathematical fact. But if we have a clear grasp of that presence ourselves and we seek consistently to present it and to point to it, even many who will query our judgment on any specific incident will learn over the years to listen to what we have to say and to look twice where our finger is pointing.

This is how we help lost man to recognize his God. It is also how we assist God to establish his presence among men. When we have said that, we must go on next to see how we achieve it in practice.

Jesus achieved it by teaching in parables, and this, too, must be one of our methods. While I don't want to ignore all that the New Testament scholars have said about the parables and the teaching of Jesus, no more do I want at this juncture to get involved in their arguments. Instead, and without doing harm to any of the main principles of parabolic interpretation, I want to focus attention on what I consider to be the significant points for preachers.

What Jesus was doing with his parables was enabling people to "see" or to "perceive," and the people who wandered around after him were treated to a string of stories, tales, and anecdotes which were not all of one type. Some of them were human stories, possibly current coin at that time, but which Jesus retold either to give them a slight twist of meaning, to bring out a point that others seemed to be missing, or to enable people to see the familar thing in a fresh light. Some of them were simply built-up illustrations of truth, sometimes prompted by local circumstances and sometimes prompted by questions from the audience. But I take the point of them all to be that expressed by Jesus himself in Mark 4:11-12:

> "To you has been given the secret of the kingdom of God, but for those outside everything is in parables; so that they may indeed see but not perceive, and may indeed hear but not understand; lest they should turn again, and be forgiven."

In other words, there are many people to whom the preacher's parable will be nonsense; there are others to whom it will be just a good story. But by holding it up in front of people and by directing their attention to it, and possibly also by the context in which we set it, we shall make it possible for one here and another there "to see the light." Without our word people may see but not perceive, may hear the words and miss the Word.

Ursula Wolfel, in a volume of stories to think about, tells the story of Johnny, who was missing at the end of a school outing. When the teacher inquired of the other children, nobody had seen him. When pressed further, some of them thought he hadn't even set off with them. He was so quiet and he never had a friend. But when it grew dark, their fears for Johnny increased until all at once they saw him coming toward the bus with the teacher and the bus driver who had gone to look for him. Nothing at all had gone wrong. He'd just strayed to cut a stick, and the others had all gone on and left him without noticing. When he was safely in the bus and digging into his rucksack, he suddenly looked up and asked,

> "Why are you all staring at me like that?"
> "What? Oh, nothing," they said.
> And one of them called out: "You've got ever such a lot of freckles on your nose!"
> And they all laughed, including Johnny.
> "But I've always had those," he said.[1]

To begin with, it's a good story and as such is well worth reading or telling. To those with only a little imagination it has a point—perhaps several points. We miss so much of what is around us all the time. We don't notice people until they are in trouble. We lose contact with people very easily and only with difficulty can we reestablish it, and so on. Each of these interpretations, however, depends on our seeing the story from the point of view of the children in the bus. A "Johnny," listening to the story, would immediately identify with the boy in the story and see something quite different.

The preacher who wishes to "use" it, as Jesus "used" his stories, can take it even further. He will decide just what he wants the story to say, but instead of telling his congregation he will link the story with a passage of Scripture or (less likely) a hymn and perhaps even follow it with a sermon on some subject, such as "Our Business Is Persons." That story can then be used in such a way as to point out the contrast between what we say and what we do. If the preacher is really skillful, he will choose a week when perhaps some local person has taken an overdose and there has been a lot of publicity. We are all terribly concerned! But did we ever really notice the man until he was desperate?

Preaching in this way is doing far more than relating stories and proclaiming ideas. It is holding up a picture, at a certain angle and in a certain context, so as to relate to some emotion that is already present in the heart of the hearer. Such seed falls then into fruitful ground, and the Word strikes home.

That is a verbal picture, such as Jesus used, but nowadays, especially with a small congregation, there is scope for the use of photographic material for the same purpose.

About once a month, for example, you have an article in the press on the future of our cities, the wasteful society that we are, or the future of young people. Choose one or two key sentences to set the scene and acquaint people with the problem and use them to introduce the theme to the worshiper early in the service in the Act of Preparation. Then produce a picture, slide, or photograph which embodies all these topics.

After the Act of Preparation, confront worshipers with the visual aid and have a dialogue. You might begin by asking questions:

What does this picture mean?

What does it say to YOU?

What is this person in the picture thinking?

What is this person feeling?

Is this a picture of hope or despair?

The dialogue may begin as a conversation between the preacher and a few members, but it will easily become a dialogue between the worshipers themselves as they see different things and register different impressions while gazing at the same picture.

The preacher who knows his theology will know before he begins that it is a mark of the man in Christ that he sees hope when others see despair, and that it is a mark of natural man that he sees despair where others see hope, but he will not say so. Instead, by use of a visual aid, he will carefully lead members of his congregation until they face a choice between seeing hope or despair. He will then proceed to read a biblical passage which will make clear what we believe about hope and fear so that people, already clearly committed to a point of view, will judge themselves. That is how it was in the New Testament.

Not everybody will see the connection. Not all who see it will admit it, even to themselves. That also is how it was in the New Testament. But even if the preacher fails in this way, he would probably never have succeeded in getting through with words. And if he succeeds, he has not simply succeeded in conveying ideas to a person after which that person has to translate the ideas into action, but rather he has already brought about a change in a man. His very method has ensured that he himself was used as a vehicle of the Holy Spirit.

The whole operation may be over in no more than five minutes, but if it changes a person and is the beginning of perception, it will point up something richer and deeper that is to follow.

Current songs, pop or folk, are often parables for those with ears to hear, and they need only a little sharpening up or a particular context in order to strike home. A preacher may begin here simply to show what God is saying in the world, but once the point is grasped, he can go on to explore its depth and relevance for those who want meat and not sweetmeat.

When there was a current song, "I'd rather be a hammer than a nail," I asked my Sunday morning congregation early in the service which they would prefer to be, and not surprisingly most of them readily identified as hammers. This is partly because nobody wants to be a nail, but it is also because anyone who feels like a nail keeps quiet when the hammers are preparing for action. Without any further comment we then read 1 Samuel 11 where Saul at Gibeah hears that the people of Jabesh-gilead are being threatened by the Ammonites. Saul immediately cut up a yoke of oxen, sent them throughout Israel with messengers, and said, "Whoever does not come out after Saul and Samuel, so shall it be done to his oxen!" That was followed by the story of the stoning of Stephen (Acts 7). In this way hammer and nail were identified in Scripture, and members of the congregation began to see themselves more clearly and to be happy (or unhappy) with their attitudes.

For many, this much would be sufficient, and the sound of the familiar song would be a reminder in the following week, but there were others who were able to go further. The sermon therefore identified hammers and nails in other places, such as politics, industry, or education. What emerged from this interpretation was that the nail is not necessarily a weak or feeble character, but it performs a different role. He is made of the same stuff but uses his strength to hold things together rather than to impose his will on others. When he is reviled, he reviles not again! David, both at Ziph and at Engedi, had a chance to hammer Saul, but he refrained because this was not the way he saw life and victory. The nail takes the blows as they come, and it is only a short step from this kind of description to a picture of Jesus as the perfect nail.

We asked what makes a hammer, and in this case we found the answer in the second verse of the same song, "I'd rather be a sparrow than a snail." The sparrow devours the snail because it needs the snail to maintain its own existence, however superior to the snail it may appear on the surface. Saul felt like that about David and that is why he hit him. Every hammer needs a nail, as a teacher needs a pupil, a doctor needs a patient, and a businessman needs a competitor. Two hammers are no use at all. Two nails could be demolished by anyone. But a hammer and a nail make a good partnership. And so from simple beginnings some people have been brought right through to the matter of relationships.

What now is the worshiper to make of himself—either as a hammer or a nail? The only answer is the one which the worshiper himself supplies, and it will be different for every individual, but the preacher has enabled the Word to get through in its own way; and each time the song comes up during the following week, the Word has a further chance to strike home again and again.

A more imaginative preacher might like at some point to use the passage from *Jesus Christ—Superstar* where they are hammering in the nails. This would suggest that the Jewish authorities were a hammer and Jesus was a nail, and so add a new dimension. Further reference could be made to Stephen, and prayer time could be an opportunity to ask the congregation to suggest "hammers and nails" who need our prayers.

A church with good visual facilities could get across the same points and many others by a selective use of cartoon features. "Tom and Jerry" are living embodiments of the hammer and the nail and reveal a good strong relationship in a way that an inanimate hammer and nail never can. But Tom and Jerry also show how the little one finally comes out on top. Christianity, too, is about this— the victory of the underdog, and the way in which God can use the despised and the rejected. Linked with Isaiah 53, a cartoon like this can take on new depth.

Moreover, a preacher who pursues this line steadily will instill in his congregation a new sense of hearing and seeing. He will have established the presence of God in their lives and will have made them aware. From now on life will increasingly take on a new dimension, and all sorts of fresh possibilities will have opened up. The Word has got through and established itself.

The preacher who regards this as "kids' stuff" may well be right, but he should not despise it on that account. For one thing there are many adults who function all their lives at this level, as is evidenced by the literature they read and the programs they watch, and we do them no service if we insist on functioning only on a level that is acceptable in the seminar. Moreover, we have scriptural authority for becoming as little children, bearing in mind that the child often has a capacity for insight that puts the adult to shame.

However, if the straight service and sermon is to be followed, the same basic concept can still be kept, and the preacher who wishes to do this will get great help from the world of drama, the novel, and the theater. Books like *The Ark of God* by Douglas Stewart, *Speak What We Feel* by Kay Baxter, and *Guard Our Unbelief* by J. J. Evans[2] all have much to contribute at this point in helping the preacher who is new to this territory to see the wood for the trees. Choose a play which is on at the local theater, on radio or television, or which your people might recently have seen but not perceived. Settle for the thrust of its message and let that be your theme. Use your knowledge of the Bible, theology, and life to light it up and then let it speak for itself.

To continue the same theme, take John Osborne's *Look Back in Anger* as an example.[3] The two central characters are Jimmy and Alison Porter. Jimmy is a bear, and a very angry bear at that, who growls at everything. The more he feels threatened, the more noise he makes. Alison, his wife, is a timid squirrel. He's had a hard life and it's made him what he is. She's had a very easy life and it's never really made her anything at all. They are so different that the marriage, not unexpectedly, is very rough. Sometimes they just resolve their differences by playing a little game in which he pretends to be a bear and she pretends to be a squirrel.

I wouldn't dwell on this theme very much, but if I thought the play was just in the consciousness of some members of the congregation, I would bring it to the surface by a sermon on "Bears and Squirrels." Jeremiah was a bear. Hosea was a squirrel. Put them together and see what happens. Throw in a couple of

politicians or public figures who that week have been fighting—
one has been growling and the other has been quietly suffering.
Try to show how each character has its place. What would happen
to all the social reforms if there were no bears about? What would
life be like if everybody had a social reforming zeal? Bring it even
nearer home. Show how this balance keeps many marriages
together.

By this stage some members of the congregation have been
trapped! They have been conned into a line where they saw
themselves as bears or squirrels (hammers or nails); and suddenly
when you mention marriage, the discussion takes on a new
dimension. It is no longer academic—it is real. This may be the
point to introduce Jimmy and Alison Porter and to show how they
need each other, and perhaps the place to finish is by showing that
the only person who has succeeded in integrating both aspects in
himself is Jesus.

All this is the stuff of preaching, and the same points can be
found in a dozen places for the preacher who is clear what he is
looking for and knows how to keep his eyes and ears open. This is a
very different approach from that which says that the preacher
should use contemporary material. That may mean nothing more
than deciding exactly what you want to say and then casting
around for contemporary incidents to illustrate or bolster up the
argument. What we are advocating here is a form of preaching
which is prepared to look at contemporary events to see what they
are saying, and then to interpret them in the light of Scripture and
theology. It is learning to look under every stone and ask, "What is
God doing here?" Bible and theology are certainly not bypassed,
but like all good foundations, provided they are there and doing
their job, they need not always be all that much in evidence.

The preacher who handles this approach well will also find that
before long members of his congregation are after him for the
recipe. Let them see a little, and like the disciples they will come
back and say, "Lord, teach us to pray." For what we are talking
about is prayer. It is communication with the eternal. There is
therefore a case for "cooking lessons"—sessions in church where
you allow your method to come under the microscope and the
congregation is allowed to see what is happening. We will take just
one way of doing this to illustrate what we mean.

Peter Berger says that although people seem not to believe in the supernatural as they once did, they are nevertheless surrounded by signals of transcendence. (See page 82 of this book.) These signals are phenomena in our natural environment which appear to point beyond that environment. Commitment to their existence is an admission that there is more to life than can be seen on a casual acquaintance. To listen to what the signals say indicates a willingness to listen to God. Berger suggests five such signals: the world of play, order, humor, hope, and damnation.[4]

The "cooking lesson" therefore takes the form of an inquiry into each of these worlds to see what it has to say. A group of students in a college might be the best place to begin, but there is no reason why a group of church members should not do it. Ask them to take one of Berger's five signals and then to collect evidence to support it from books, newspapers, songs, pictures, and anywhere else. In our case we had a group which worked at this for a whole winter and produced four services, one on each theme (with hope and damnation being handled together). Subsequently, the same group produced a thirty-minute television program using some of the best material from each of the services.

In the world of play, for example, we began with a call to worship which was a 60-second tape called "Sounds of play"—a baby's rattle, a football cheer, an aria, a motorbike being revved up, applause, music, etc. We sang a hymn. We watched a short film of some children at play, and we read the familiar Scripture from Mark about becoming like little children. All this created something of the atmosphere and an impression of the world with which we were dealing.

We then read a short extract from *The Little Prince*[5] which really brought us into the world of the child, for it showed the little prince asking simple but nevertheless awkward questions of a businessman whose main preoccupation is counting the stars. The little prince is so "simple" and so persistent that at the end of the reading the congregation cannot help but be aware that there are two ways of looking at life—the way of the businessman and the way of the child. Some of them will begin to see cracks in a system which up to that minute they had accepted without question.

From there you could go on to point out that in fact we all live in both worlds. It may be 10:30 P.M. in the real world, but in the world of play for the fifteen-year-old girl it's the last kiss; in the center of the city it may be time for the last bus, and in the theater it's the last act of the play with all of its tension and climactic discovery.

There is poetry and song which all belong to the theme and which any experimental group could bring together, but in the end it should be made quite clear to everyone that though all the pressures of the Western world are geared to make us live like businessmen who count the stars as well as their money, it is very often only in the moments when we learn to play and to wonder that we touch eternity. A congregation which sees this truth in church will then become more sensitive to it in the world.

Michel Quoist's prayer, "I Like Youngsters,"[6] will further enable people to feel that though they had never realized it before, it is some of these great moments of play that are the real moments of life—these are the moments when they are nearest to God. If this insight comes through, then the presence of God has been established in a place where hitherto he had not been noticed.

A similar batch of material could then be collected relating to the theme of order, showing how man seems to have a basic instinct to impose order on material, how groups which claim to reject order are very often rejecting only one form of order, how those who break away from established patterns very often end up by imposing (or discovering) another kind of order. In this respect we came across a group of people who twenty years earlier had rejected the concept of the Western family pattern in favor of the kibbutz, but after twenty years some mothers were keeping their babies with them at night instead of leaving them in the dormitory, on the grounds that babies need their mothers! (Or was it that mothers needed their babies?) Some members of the kibbutz even cooked meals in their quarters instead of going to the refectory, and so on.

This story then raised the question as to whether order is simply human or whether it is something that transcends the human. A group may look for similar examples in the animal kingdom. Finally this led us to confront the congregation with the question: When you see the forces of order all around you, do you want to say that the ultimate end of all order is God? If you do, wherever you submit to order or cooperate with order, God may not be very far away. So once again, you have staked a claim for the presence of God.

Humor threatened to be the most difficult of all to handle until we read that Dr. Thomas Trotter, Dean of Claremont Divinity School, had described Charlie Chaplin as the prime theologian of our time because he made a sacrament of laughter. Chaplin, he said, is a living commentary on 1 Corinthians 13—patient and kind, doesn't insist on his own way, is not resentful, doesn't rejoice in the wrong, but rejoices in the right, believes all things, hopes all things, endures all things. Then he added that amid all the other things that were happening in the 1930s, filling the newspapers and providing the main topics of conversation in the shops and on the buses, in the pubs and in the pulpits, it is these Chaplin-like characteristics that have survived. The very existence of a clown is the messenger of God.

A further look at the clown shows something of his ability to match the unpredictable and disorderly events of life, like falling ladders and oncoming trains, with grace, wit, and humor. Because of this he has the ability to change life and relationships.

When I was in college, one of the "treatments" for a man who got too big for his boots was to strip his room. It happened to one of my colleagues one Saturday. Every bit of furniture and every article of clothing had been taken out and stowed away in other parts of the building. He came back late that Saturday night; and as he climbed the stairs, the silence was broken only by the breathing of those who knew what to expect and waited for it. He threw open the door, switched on the light and. . . . There were three things he could have done. One was to storm about and annoy everybody else. The second was quietly to find a couple of friends to help him to restore order and say nothing to anybody else. He did neither. He simply let out an enormous laugh as if his sides would split, and in no time half-a-dozen fellows were at his elbow helping him to put things back. The clown was out, and the situation was transformed.

Other groups may wish to dwell on the way the poor clown has to go on clowning even when his heart is breaking, and a good illustration of that is Jack Point, as he unburdens himself to Wilfred in Gilbert and Sullivan's *The Yeoman of the Guard.* Others may wish to relate the theme to clowns for Christ in 1 Corinthians 1:18-29 and to see the preacher as a clown. But whatever angle is chosen, the ultimate of all the material is to establish the presence of God in the world of humor and to enable people to hear his voice.

Material on the theme of damnation and hope is at hand in all the press. There are some situations in life so evil that you feel they just cannot be tolerated. They must be stopped immediately. And if man doesn't stop them, then some higher power must be invoked. Some people sense this when they are confronted with the death of a child or a natural disaster or even a suffering animal. But equally people find that the very same experience often leads also to the emergence of hope. Both characteristics seem to point to something beyond oneself.

A story which is relevant in this context is that of Martin Gray.[7] It begins with the Jews in Germany in the 1930s. When the Germans marched into Poland, Jews were excluded from all the professions. The Jews had accepted this, and at least nobody was killing them; so they put up with it. Then they were forced to wear an armband bearing the Star of David—and they accepted this because they were not ashamed of being Jews. Then came the ghetto—and they accepted this because they were with their own kind and they were saved from Polish hooliganism. Next came three years of starvation before the Nazis started shipping them out to a concentration camp.

At Treblinka everything was done with supreme efficiency. A single-line railway track ended only a stone's throw from the gas chambers. It was all so cool—even at the end the victims thought they were going for a bath, and the Germans played music to cover up the screams of the dying.

When you read a story like that—even after thirty years—you are left with the feeling that here is something man can never get away with. And even to say that is to reach out for some sort of ultimate condemnation of ultimate evil. It is a cry to a good God.

Yet it is in this evil situation that hope is born. With all the odds loaded against him, Martin Gray had the job of sorting out the clothes of the exterminated prisoners, of carrying the still-warm bodies of the children from the gas chambers to the common grave. And yet he had enough hope to escape; and when he went to tell his fellow-Poles the truth, they were the first to rebel.

After the war Martin Gray escaped to America and made a fortune. He married Dina, a Dutch girl, and at the ripe old age of thirty-five he was able to retire to the south of France. There he lived in a beautiful farmhouse with 150 acres of land and gorgeous views of the Mediterranean. Then, in a forest fire, he lost his wife and his four children. Like Job, he saw his whole family wiped out before his eyes. Unlike Job, he didn't bless the Lord. Indeed, in his book he points out gently that not once does he refer to God. But if his book is not written in praise of God, in fact God is not very far away. Gray's story is the story of the indomitability of the human spirit—the spirit shot through with life eternal. He has encountered more horrors than most people would encounter in ten lifetimes, and still he has a dogged determination to survive.

His determination is more than merely to survive. He has now given his life to the Dina Gray Foundation, concerned with educating children to the dangers of forest fires. He is hoping to remarry and start again. When asked about it, he said, "I don't want to talk about that, except to say that I could never live without giving life. Without that I would die."

If a man can live like that, can God be far away? And if the preacher can establish in the minds of his hearers an awareness of God in situations of this sort, then he has succeeded in confronting them with the incarnation—God in flesh. His sessions on *A Rumor of Angels* will have taken on the shape of a "cook's kitchen" where people have been taught to cook for themselves and are then equipped to go out and share their insights with others.

This is not the whole of the gospel, any more than the parables are the whole of the gospel, but it's certainly on the way. In the pattern of worship it belongs to the earlier part of the service where we are concerned with the Word, though (as we have seen) it may pass over at times directly to the sermon, but it is part of the experience of Isaiah where he says,

> Then flew one of the seraphim to me, having in his hand a burning coal which he had taken with tongs from the altar. And he touched my mouth, and said: "Behold, this has touched your lips; your guilt is taken away, and your sin forgiven" (Isaiah 6:6-7).

If the first step in worship and preaching is an awareness of our lost state, the second is the sense of cleansing and hope which the living Word provides. It is a continual awareness of this presence that leads us to look for a miracle and a mission.

A
SAVING
PRESENCE

If preaching begins with finding a person who is lost and God's coming to him in the incarnation, then the next thing we must expect to happen is that such a person's life will be changed. When Paul became aware of the presence of God on the Damascus Road, the first thing he had to do was to obey the command to go on into Damascus and wait; but he hadn't been there long before his whole life was turned inside out. All this is part of what we understand by preaching. The change that takes place in a person's life is not to be seen as the result of preaching, any more than an awareness of God's presence is to be called a preparation for preaching, for it is through both that God communicates.

It is worth our while to return to Moses at this point because Moses is in many respects a forerunner of Jesus. Moses communicates his understanding of God to his people, first simply by being present among them and then, secondly, by delivering them from slavery. He doesn't preach to them until they respond before he delivers them; he preaches and communicates by effecting the deliverance. Indeed, in these early stages of man's understanding of God it is the act itself that not only demonstrates God's presence but shows also what kind of God he is. He is one who requires people to turn their backs on the past, to *behave* as free men even though they *know* they are slaves. Then God becomes for them the One who takes the ultimate obstacle (the Red Sea) and turns it into his opportunity. Let a man experience that and he has begun to believe in a God who will do anything.

Similarly with Jesus. He is not simply a presence to show people where they are wrong and how they can be put right. That was the role played by John the Baptist, and it is regrettable that the church in her preaching has often followed John more than Jesus. Jesus is more concerned to achieve the transformation that he talked about—actually to find the lost and to deliver them from slavery—and this he did by miracles. Miracle is an appropriate method because preaching is concerned with salvation, and man's salvation is always a miracle.

The miracles, like the parables, were of varied kinds, and I am not anxious to stop at this juncture and say precisely what happened or what it meant, but I take the message of the miracles to be that Jesus proclaims by doing and not just by telling. When he is around, blind men do see, lame men do walk, tepid water does become super wine, and so on. Even death is never the end that the unbelieving observer assumes it to be. Like Moses, Jesus enables people to turn their backs on the past, to *behave* as if they are free even though they know they are bound (the cripple has to take up his bed and walk), and to take the ultimate obstacle (death) and turn it into a basis for hope. Furthermore, Jesus does not do all this or point to all this and simply ask people to believe in it—he brings about the change by his presence, and the people believe as they are saved, instead of being saved as they believe.

It is in some such way that our preaching must work miracles and our miracles will be our preaching. It is not enough to talk about the blind seeing—it must actually happen in the congregation. So-and-so who has been blind and stubborn on that point for years must suddenly be seen to see! It is not enough to talk about the lame walking—that must happen, too! So-and-so who has dragged his feet for years over something or other must actually be seen to be walking and running and thrilled that he is no longer held back by whatever it was that gripped him. It is not enough even to *talk* about the resurrection! And so the church itself which has always been afraid of changing this or surrendering that must be seen to be patterning its life in such a way that it has thrown off all of its old body and has risen to newness of life with a new body; for it is in this very transformation, plain for all to see, that God is communicated.

To act in this way is to preach and to proclaim a miracle-working risen Christ; and when such things are happening, not many words are necessary. At the same time we would not want to drive a wedge between word and action, for Word and Sacrament belong together, and therefore we must go on to discover how we can preach by miracles.

To achieve this end, we have to begin a long way back. People have lost the sense of miracle to such an extent that if they were to see one, the first thing they would do would be to look for an explanation. Many more have lost the sense of miracle to such an extent that they would not even recognize one. Therefore the first thing we have to do is to give people dreams and visions to establish in them a sense of wonder or mystery and to build up confidence and trust.

There is a good parallel to our contemporary condition in Exodus 6:9, where Moses makes an early approach to his people and the Bible says, "They did not listen to Moses, because of their broken spirit and their cruel bondage." You might have thought that in their state they would have been only too glad to listen, but what Moses was talking about was so far from the conditions they were living in that it had no meaning. It was as meaningless a word as is color to a man born blind. But when Moses stopped talking to them and there followed a series of miraculous events called plagues, culminating in the most miraculous event of all, the deliverance of the firstborn, then the people caught a vision of what was possible and they were ready for more. Without that experience the crossing of the Red Sea may not have been possible, and even if that did come about, without the vision it is doubtful whether they would have appreciated it and interpreted it in the same way.

This lack of vision or expectation is the lot of oppressed people in many parts of the world today; it is the lot of many ministers and members in some of our urban areas, and of many women who are tied to the kitchen sink. It is possible maybe to hold their attention with stories of miracles—of drug addicts and alcoholics who have come to new life—but all the time they will see the miracle as something that happens somewhere else to somebody else. But create in them some sense of wonder at what God is doing and they will begin to feel the possibility of miracle for them.

A good example of a dream that became a springboard for hope is the story of Carolina Maria de Jesus, a Negro woman who lived with her three illegitimate children in the slums of Sao Paulo in

Brazil. It was all she could do to keep body and soul together, but she had a burning passion to write. She went around the garbage cans collecting scraps of paper on which to write a diary. Here was a woman in slavery, but whose dreams enabled her to transcend the situation and conceive of something better.

Two short passages indicate how, to begin with, the dream seemed to accentuate her slavery and yet how the dream also was the occasion of her deliverance.

> I spent a horrible night. I dreamt I lived in a decent house that had a bathroom, kitchen, pantry and even a maid's room. . . . I went and bought some small pots that I had wanted for a long time. Because I was able to buy. I sat at the table to eat. The tablecloth was white as a lily. I ate a steak, bread and butter, fried potatoes, and a salad. When I reached for another steak I woke up. What bitter reality! I don't live in the city. I live in the favela. In the mud on the banks of the Tietê River.[1]

But then,

> . . . When I was writing I was in a golden palace, with crystal windows and silver chandeliers. My dress was finest satin and diamonds sat shining in my black hair. Then I put away my book and the smells came in through the rotting walls and rats ran over my feet. My satin turned to rags and the only things shining in my hair were lice.[2]

Compare that with the man who said, "Lord, if you will, you can make me clean" (Luke 5:12). He, too, had dreamed of the possibility of being made clean and it only accentuated his condition, but that same dream led him to demand and to claim that possibility when Jesus was around. Effective preaching therefore is conveying to people the possibilities that await them in such a way that they will be ready to go out and claim them, like free men and women. The miracle is the child of simple trust, but a mature faith and an understanding of God are the children of the miracle.

One man in literature who has made this discovery is Tom in Tennessee Williams' play, *The Glass Menagerie*.[3] The point is made so succinctly that a preacher would do well to see (or read) the play and then ask himself in what ways he could proclaim the same truth. I did it once in a sermon, "Escape from a Coffin," in which I never mentioned the play, though those who had seen the play in town that week didn't need two guesses as to where the theme had come from.

There is one speech where Tom tells his mother and crippled

sister, who have in fact some kind of nagging hold over him, how he went to the theater and saw a magician with a large box invite members of the audience to nail him inside. He got the volunteers; they nailed him in; and then the magician got out. Tom says that it's impossible—nobody can escape from a coffin! And it is just at that moment that he has a flash of insight. He realizes that this is exactly what his father had done. Only his father had never died. He, too, had been nagged by Tom's mother, and when family life got too much for him, he had escaped from "the coffin" in which he was trapped simply by walking out into the unknown. And he had never been seen since.

Tom knows this is just what he has wanted to do for years and has never seen it as a possibility. Now that he has seen it, he can go, and he does, just like the Hebrews before him. They didn't think they could escape either until one of them set off; they followed and proved it true. It was much the same with many of the things that Jesus did and taught. People had always assumed there were things you just couldn't do, until he did them. And they knew that if you hit something really hard and killed it, that would be the end. Jesus said it wouldn't, and it wasn't! The end was the beginning and the grave was the scene of birth.

If the preacher wants to see changed lives, therefore, his first task must be to enable people to see what is possible and to help them to realize that they can go out and claim it. They must begin to see that miracles can happen.

There is a reflection of this same point from a different angle when Harvey Cox says that "Adam is the Everyman who at first will not and then cannot be a man."[4] Instead he is content to let a snake tell him what to do, whereas Jesus is fully man in the sense that he is prepared to take full responsibility for his actions as God intended that he should. Similarly, Paul says that although the forces that impair human responsibility are great, no one *has* to be determined by them. "Man may be free—if he chooses to be."[5] It is because this is so that we can control our lives and our cities—and unless we believe this, no miracles are likely to happen.

Preaching like this brings people to the point where the door is open. Only a few will go through and claim what is theirs, but unless the door is constantly seen to be open and attention is drawn to what lies beyond, nothing will happen at all. Preaching may be words, but it won't be action.

Once the hearer begins to move out through the door, or at least to show an interest in what goes on there, then the preacher's next task is to be ready to interpret the changes (miracles, maybe) that are already taking place. The prerequisite for doing this is the conviction on the part of the preacher that wherever miracles are happening for the benefit of mankind God is behind them. It's a question of seeing God as on our side.

An ancient Greek legend tells how when Sisyphus died and went down into the underworld, he was compelled to roll a stone uphill. But before it reached the top of the hill, the stone always rolled down, and Sisyphus had to begin all over again. I used to see that story as a man being punished by the gods for his wickedness, and I suspect that is how the Greeks meant it to be seen. But I think now I would prefer to see it as a man rebelling against his lot. Sisyphus was determined not to surrender to what fate prescribed for him. There was something inside him which prevented him from giving in, and if it was the Greek gods who had prescribed the punishment, then it was the Christian God who supplied the spirit of nonsurrender. The difference is that the Greeks saw God as somebody who was on the other side. Jesus showed God as somebody who is on our side, helping us to battle against the forces that would crush us; and when we win, it is not we who win but Christ who triumphs in us. I think this is what Paul meant when he said, "It is no longer I who live, but Christ who lives in me" (Galatians 2:20).

David Anderson interprets Camus, the novelist, as one who has worked this out, and there is much mileage here for the preacher. He works out two kinds of rebellion: there is "the false, self-destroying kind which is rebellion *against* God; and the true, liberating and life-giving kind which is rebellion *with* God."[6] If we want to effect changes and work miracles, we have to see ourselves as rebels with God, and we have to see Jesus Christ as the greatest rebel of us all. When we fight evil, we don't fight alone; we fight in company with God. It is only this awareness which gives us hope for believing that change is possible and worth interpreting when it happens.

When we go on to look at the miracles worked by Jesus, we notice that the blind began to see, the dumb began to speak, the lame began to walk, and so on. The temptation is to say, "It doesn't happen now—if it did, I would believe." But this is a false argument. In the time of Jesus only a few believed. Nevertheless, what Jesus did was to demonstrate by his miracles that God was on their side. When Jesus enables a man to overcome his disability and to start a new life, he is helping him to a discovery of a new image of God. Instead of seeing a God who was on the other side and who punished him for being evil, man suddenly becomes aware of God as being on his side. It is in fact the precise reversal of what went wrong in Genesis 1-2.

The preacher therefore will learn to spot the places where this is happening and to alert people to what it means. Miracles, in fact, are no fewer than in the time of Jesus, but many, even among the regular worshipers, miss them, often because they are too busy looking for direct replicas of what Jesus did. Broadly speaking, in this respect, there are two types of miracles to look for.

First, there is the miracle of discovery and invention that enables people to overcome their limitations. This was brought home to one congregation when the minister planned a service on overcoming handicaps, with special reference to physical disabilities. A young fellow with very restricted physical ability demonstrated a piece of equipment known as POSSUM. The letters stand for Patient Operated Selector Mechanisms (P.O.S.M.), slightly altered so as to be known by "Possum," the Latin for "I can," because POSSUM enables people to do for themselves operations which previously they had been able to do only with the help of others. In this case, the only movement the man had was in one hand, but this was sufficient to stop and start his wheelchair. The other thing he could do was to suck and blow, and with the help of his electronic POSSUM he was able to steer. POSSUM also enabled him to type and to run a small accountancy business. It was the same device that enabled Hilary Pole, whose only movement was in one big toe, to write letters and poetry and to communicate with her friends, for, unlike the young man, Hilary was unable even to talk without POSSUM.[7]

All this is miracle. It is the sort of miracle that enables people to "walk," even if not literally, and it is a miracle that needs to be proclaimed as the action of God in the world. It proclaims a God who is concerned for our well-being, and it is far more meaningful than the sort of proclamation which is preoccupied with why God doesn't do this, that, or the other. Moreover, there are many other "miracles" to cope with other disabilities, such as blindness and deafness and mental limitations. Indeed over a period of time, a whole series of services could be held on the miracles that enable us to overcome handicaps.

Secondly, there is the miracle of the human spirit. This enables people to overcome where the circumstances cannot be changed. Not all the lepers in the time of Jesus were cleansed, and not all the widows of Nain had their sons restored to them. There were many who just had to live with their limitations, and any triumph was a spiritual triumph.

Here again there are good examples at hand, but preachers often miss them, in some cases because they are too busy looking for miracles of restoration and in other cases because these people do not always subscribe to the formulas of Christian doctrine. But there is no New Testament evidence to suggest that if a person overcame without holding traditional doctrines, that miracle was any less the work of God. What made a miracle the work of God was the faith of the evangelist who enabled others to see God in action.

There are people in every parish who have overcome handicaps, and it is a good idea to seek them out and talk to them in the context of worship, for about five minutes or so, about their lives and the way they have overcome. I tried it with a woman who had been blind from birth, and for my last question I asked her whether she ever felt resentful. She said she had often felt resentment, but she had noticed that when you did a jigsaw puzzle, you often picked up a peculiarly shaped piece that seemed to fit nowhere. Yet the puzzle was never complete without it! And that was how she saw herself as a member of society despite her limitations. On the surface this may appear very different from the usual sort of testimony, and in a way it is. But in another way it isn't, because there is something liberating about a person who has overcome. His freedom literally opens the door for other people to find their freedom, in much the same way that our Lord's resurrection brought about a change on the part of the disciples and opened new doors for them and for others.

But invention and creativity on the part of man know no bounds, and it is this that the preacher needs to recognize, to claim for God, and to interpret. Not everybody will agree. Some will say these things are the devil's work, like those religious beings in the New Testament who said, "He casts out demons by the prince of demons" (see Mark 3:22). Some will take no notice and say, "That has nothing to do with God—it's just man," like those others in the New Testament who said, "Is not this the son of Joseph, the carpenter, and are not his mother and brothers here with us?" But a few (see Matthew 13:55) will come to see the miracle as the hand of God, and that act of faith and belief will change their lives.

For those then who are prepared to listen we can go one stage further. We can explain in more detail how this miracle comes about.

Here the crucial factor is somebody's willingness to exercise his priesthood, which means he must be willing to take responsibility for others and, if need be, to die for others. Moses had to be ready to take responsibility for all that went wrong in Sinai, and in the end he had to accept the fact that no benefits of the Promised Land were to be made available to him, though he would have the joy of seeing others enter in. Jesus, similarly, had to die in order that others might live, and the wonder of the resurrection I take to be much more the life of faith that appeared in others as a result of his death than anything that subsequently happened to his body.

Therefore, if we are to effect transformation by our preaching, we must create situations where people can die; and if we are to make this plain to people, we must always be ready to put our spotlight on those situations where death has been the gateway to life.

A good theatrical presentation of this theme is to be found in the musical *Hair,* which was full of theological content and regrettably dismissed by too many as if it were no more than an American version of the Paris Follies. Its message is dulled now only because the war in Vietnam is over.

Hair is a musical "be-in" with bells, beads, incense, flowers, wild costumes, and fantasy dreams. It is popularly seen as a protest against the draft in the U.S.A. and portrays American youth burning their draft cards and turning to drugs. Act 1 raises the question "Where do I go?" which is a profoundly religious question, and the one person who least understands how to answer it is Claude. He is one of the few who hasn't burned his draft cards, and to this extent he stands out from the others.

In Act 2, Claude joins the others in a drug trip in which he sees a sort of pageant of American history with all its killing, and this leads into the song, "How Dare They End This Beauty?" By now our eyes are wide open. All of the participants have a drive to escape, but Claude wishes he were invisible and could perform miracles. He wants to be a hermit and hang on a cross. At this point he disappears; but when next we see him, he is in uniform. "They got me," he says; "I feel like I died." In the end he does die, and a cross is held up over his body.

My first thought when I saw it was that here was a man who came to see that if he were to enjoy the benefits for which his forefathers had fought, then he, too, must be willing to fight and die for them. This may be, on reflection, too positive a view. It could just be that they got him and crucified him, but in any case the connection with the New Testament is too close, for it is not certain that even Jesus saw all too clearly what it was all about. He knew he had a responsibility, and he carried it through even to the point of death. It was really only afterwards that it all became clear.

And is it not true that even in Claude's case there was a resurrection? In *Hair* there is a hint at this in the final song, "Let the Sun Shine In." In real life, is it not true that the death of Claude (American youth) more than anything else changed the attitude of America toward Vietnam. This is how the miracle of transformation is achieved—only when someone is willing to die.

It doesn't matter that the preacher hasn't seen *Hair* and that the war in Vietnam is over. Once he begins to see this concept clearly, he will see it literally everywhere, and life and preaching will take on a new dimension. All I am trying to do is to indicate some ways in which I have been able in the last few years to relate the gospel to the events that were occupying people's minds at the time. I do not refer all the time to Scripture, but in every case the scriptural basis is there, and must always be a frame of reference—clear and seen to be clear.

For further clarification it is helpful to distinguish two kinds of death. When Robert Scott set out for the Antarctic, when Edmund Hillary set out for Everest, when Yuri Gagarin went into orbit, and when Father Damien went to live with the lepers, each in turn faced the possibility of death; and death which comes from facing the foe and courting disaster is quite different from the death which comes inevitably at the end of life, like leaves falling from a tree.

The Bible knows both kinds of death, and it is interesting to make a comparison between David and the Son of David. David was a go-getter. As a boy he stole a march over others by killing Goliath. He built up a friendship with Jonathan, exchanged armor with him, possibly as a symbol of blood brotherhood, and went on to claim the crown. When he saw Bathsheba, Uriah was the next one to die. Eventually the intriguer found that others had plotted against him and he died—the death of old age for the one who had killed so many.

The Son of David is different. He, too, made his early mark as a boy, but when, in his late twenties, his mother tried to get him to make his mark, she received a sharp rebuke. Unlike his ancestor who sought out those who would be advantageous to him, the Son of David sought out the rejects and nonentities. Unlike his ancestor whose motives and ambitions were obvious, the Son seems not to have had any ulterior motives. He was content to be.

Both produced their enemies. But whereas, when the chips were down, the father brought death to others to save his skin, the Son surrendered his skin to save others. David inflicted death to avoid dying before his time. The Son's death was something that he went out to greet in order that those whom he loved might be spared.

This willingness to die is part of the gospel; and where this occurs, the gospel is being preached and the preacher must point to it.

The week after Bobby Kennedy was assassinated, I had lunch with a Methodist layman, and the conversation turned to the Kennedys and Martin Luther King. He said he had recently been talking to some ministers and he had suggested parallels with Calvary which they couldn't see. They said that the death of Martin Luther King, for example, was an act of stupid folly and a wicked waste. To which he replied, "But was not the death of our Lord an act of stupid folly and a wicked waste?" And they said, "Oh, yes, but there was good that came out of it." And so he had to go on and spell out for them that the message of the cross was that out of stupid folly and wicked waste God always produces something good and worthwhile. Once a preacher sees this relationship, he can continually take what is happening in the world and help people to see what God is doing with it and where they ought to be looking for the next installment. It is the preacher's preoccupation with what God did two thousand years ago to the exclusion of what he is doing now more than anything else that leaves people lost and confused, weeping in the garden because they can't find him while all the time he is going before them into Galilee.

In some cases a contemporary incident is worth reflecting on for the other parallels that present themselves. The circumstances of the assassination of John Kennedy, for example, set me pondering on its significance and message to such an extent as to produce a sermon on the following Sunday morning in which the name of Kennedy was never mentioned. Indeed, it was almost a straight and dull description of a man who emerged into public life and after a few years became something of a national hero. But he never stopped to think about himself, going into the enemy camp and refusing any protection, being killed on a Friday at the hands of a few irresponsible people (as it seemed at that time) who in no way represented the feelings of the nation as a whole. "And today," I concluded, "is the third day since these things happened." The simple description of the life of Jesus and the cross was really all it was, but the events of the last three days had made it something quite different. Some even thought I was just telling the story of Kennedy.

It could have been spelled out more precisely in certain circumstances so as to enable people to appreciate the significance of the secular, but it happened to be preached in a situation where some people would have rejected such an interpretation and others might even have been offended by it. By preaching it straight, in this way, the hearer was left to find the cross only in Jesus or to begin to recognize the cross in life.

In the case of Robert Kennedy, I was able to raise more specific questions. Did this death, for example, force us to look at God once more as one who was on the side of youth and revolution rather than age and establishment? Within three years Jesus had conducted his own one-man revolution against all that the establishment stood for—bad religion, bad politics, bad morality, and rotten culture. After three years they were delighted to get rid of him; yet after two thousand years we are still seeing the results being worked out.

There were many points of contact to be explored. Both came to the world's problems from another sphere (Jesus from heaven and Kennedy from Harvard); both emerged relatively late for young revolutionaries (Jesus was thirty and Kennedy was forty); both had a rough start and retreated (Jesus across the Jordan and Kennedy from the White House to private life); both refused to be pushed

(Jesus at Cana of Galilee and Kennedy over Vietnam and the presidency); both were forced to grasp the nettle (partly by the pressure of events and partly by something inside themselves); both identified with the common man; both found the campaign short, sharp, and brutal; both left behind a dejected group of people (Jesus a few women at the cross and Kennedy a little Negro girl who said, "Suddenly there's no one left to vote for"). Once you penetrate through the news headlines and look beyond the details to see what is really happening, you are left with the question, "Is God saying anything to us through this kind of life and death?"

Kennedy's death is a further and pertinent reminder of the ready way in which God is rejected once it becomes clear to people what he is doing. Jesus came to see that it wasn't enough just to hold up the good, because people were only interested in the good as long as it didn't get in the way of anything else. It was then that he made his direct assault on Jerusalem, and it was then that it was borne in upon him how much he meant to his friends and his enemies.

Robert Kennedy had similar experiences. Anthony Howard, who knew him well, said that during his three-month presidential campaign it was borne in upon him how much he meant to deprived and dispossessed America. He had become the steward of a lot of hopes and the trustee of countless dreams. But at the same time he came to see in his defeat at Oregon how much the best of the nation's youth was beginning to reject him as a false god. But this now didn't seem to matter very much. The cause was greater than the man. He had to go forward to Jerusalem. And at that moment, he died—because wherever you have a man who is ultimately committed to his cause, death will always be his fate in a world that is evil.

All this is worth pointing out, not to suggest that Kennedy is another Christ nor yet another Savior, but to demonstrate that the cross is always more than two bits of wood on Calvary. It is the death of him who is willing to die and to court death for the sake of those whom he loves. Wherever this happens, therefore, the task of the preacher is to point to it against the background of the death of Christ.

What all these references indicate is simply that he who saves his life will lose it, and he who is willing to throw his life away will find his very sacrifice to be the gateway to new life. This is the crucial rock on which the Christian faith is built. It is what we express in our Communion service. The bread, the body of Christ or the material in which God dwells, must be broken in order that it may be remade; and the blood, the life, must be poured out in order to live. Seeing this is important, and the work of the preacher is both to point out that wherever this is happening it is the work of God, and to enable the event to inspire others to similar sacrifice.

In some cases people's lives will be changed simply by seeing this truth. In some cases their lives will be changed when they see what others have sacrificed for them. In some cases the very vision and its possibilities will enable them to lead new lives for others. Like the disciples who caught the spirit and went out prepared to live and die, some people will become new persons.

In the end the church that has become a cafeteria and a cook's kitchen must also be willing to die to produce the transformation she is proclaiming, and her death will be her greatest sermon. Only in this way can she proclaim a dying and a risen Lord. Both church and preacher must go out and *claim* their freedom instead of simply talking about it and complaining because they cannot get there. Preachers must be willing to die to their pulpits, and churches must be willing to die to their premises, and Christian communities must be willing to die to their isolation and distinctiveness. No amount of pointing to the saving presence of God in Christ will bring about the transformation in such a way as if the church is willing to lose herself. The church that can achieve this will preach the gospel in a big way.

It is in the "sermon" in worship, however, that the sermon is preached, that this word must continually be embodied, for here is the heart of the presence of power of God. This is where man must hear the call like Isaiah,

And I heard the voice of the Lord saying, "Whom shall I send, and who will go for us?" Then I said, "Here am I! Send me" (Isaiah 6:8).

OPENING
UP THE
FUTURE

At the end of the last chapter we saw how one person willing to die a sacrificial death can bring about a change in the lives of others. We can now go one stage further. When a person (or a group of persons) is willing to die a sacrificial death, he effectively demonstrates that the end is the beginning by opening up a new future. This is the basis of the Christian hope.

Once again we go back to Moses and Jesus. Moses saw hope where other people saw despair, and light where others could see only darkness. He could have preached this message forever, and people might have come to see what he was driving at and perhaps even to begin to believe that he was right, but they would not have actually committed themselves to it and felt it in their bones unless they had seen that Moses was prepared to put his belief to the test and they themselves (albeit tentatively) had begun to share the experience. In other words, they had to see that Moses was willing to go into the wilderness even if nobody went with him—that act spelled faith. But then when they followed Moses, they had to live through the experience of the Red Sea to know what it really meant to say that with God the end is the beginning. Only after this event did they really begin to believe.

Even so, the belief was shaky and uncertain, and it had to be tested many times. They needed the manna and the rock and Sinai with the covenant before they began to get the feel of a God who could offer them a future, and at each stage they had to see that Moses at least could believe. And after all that, when they got to the edge of the Promised Land, only two out of twelve had anything like the faith required to tackle Jericho; the rest went more from fear than conviction. But once again the Word proved right; and when a people pass through an experience like that, it does something to them.

For Jesus the crux was Calvary, but the real battle was fought long before when Jesus refused to take the easy route to solve his problems because he saw himself as the servant of mankind, a man with a mission. From the very beginning Jesus had shown himself to be a man with a capacity for seeing what others missed or for seeing in a new way. A cripple was not so much a man who needed to be healed as a man who needed to feel forgiveness and acceptance. A woman drawing water at an unusual hour of the day was one who was isolated from her local community and needed to be put back into it. According to an apocryphal story, attributed to Jesus in the *Hadith* or traditional literature of Islam,[1] Jesus and his disciples were once confronted with the carcass of a dog as they walked along a track. The disciples said, "How foul is the smell of this dog!" But Jesus said, "How white are his teeth!" It should therefore come as no surprise to us that when he read the stories of the Old Testament in particular, he came to a view of God as One who turned ends into beginnings.

By the time Jesus got to Calvary, therefore, he had accepted its inevitability, but he had also come to see what scholars since have discovered in the Servant Songs of Second Isaiah—that suffering and death are not simply the inevitable result of the Servant's mission but are in fact the very organ through which that mission is accomplished. The point is not simply that if a man is faithful, he will be killed—the world doesn't need a Christian to tell it that! The point is that always and everywhere men and churches and communities must be willing to die in order that a door to the future may be opened.

Because the disciples had not grasped this, they could only be mystified and confused when they saw Jesus with his face steadfastly set to go to Jerusalem with all that that implied. Yet within days even they began to see and to know that what looked on Friday like the end was now turning out to be the beginning. It was Jesus' death that brought the church to birth, and it was the blood of the martyrs of the early church that enabled her to grow.

This is what we are to understand by the resurrection—turning ends into beginnings, darkness into light, and death into life. It all begins (or should we say our understanding of it all begins) with Jesus, but it points to the Christ who is alive forever and at work in the world. Preaching is learning to see him in our contemporaries, to point people to him and his work, and to invite them to share in it by a willingness to live as if it were true.

From the mass of contemporary evidence which can be used we will select some examples.

When we referred to a man in his lost state in chapter 1 above, we said that one of the characteristics of such a man was that he was looking for exits. We can now go on to say that one of the characteristics of the man who is found is that *he learns to live without exits*.

In 1970 Alexander Solzhenitsyn won the Nobel Prize for Literature for his novel, *One Day in the Life of Ivan Denisovich.*[2] Ivan Denisovich is a Russian who has been given ten years' hard labor in a Siberian labor camp. On the day in question he is eight years through his sentence. He feels ill. He is forced up in the cold before dawn, fed, marched, counted, marched, and ordered around. He works all day, and then is brought back to camp, fed, counted, counted again, and returned to bed.

The novel demonstrates the indomitable courage of the human spirit that keeps going through years of living without exits. They are years in which every day is bracketed by the darkness before dawn and the darkness after dusk in which the prisoners march to and from work. But shining through the darkness there is a light, and it is pointless to ask whether Ivan Denisovich is a Christian or believes the correct doctrines. The light that shines is the light of his spirit, though I would want to say it is the light of the spirit of Christ working through him. This light is its own message where it occurs.

Through this experience Ivan Denisovich is opening up doors for other people. If we are to enable the Christ who is at work in his story to open doors for our congregations, then we have to rub their noses in the story until they really begin to feel what Paul felt when he said, "I have learned, in whatever state I am, to be content" (Philippians 4:11).

If we can convey this feeling to people and give them a sense of purpose in living so that they feel hope even in the most desperate situations and believe that it is worth going on even in despair because despair is the gateway to life, then preaching is no longer proclaiming a message of hope but rather the very creation of hope. This is the power of the Word as demonstrated in Jesus. Wherever he went, hope was born.

To achieve this end, the preacher must either have passed through this experience himself or at least he must be able to see it with a greater clarity than others, just as the artist needs a special eye for seeing, as much as a hand for drawing or painting. Solzhenitsyn himself had certainly had something of the experience, but in an earlier short story also he had demonstrated his capacity to see.

The story is called "The City on the Neva" and is a short descriptive piece on the beauty of Leningrad, but it has a clear message. He describes the dome of St. Isaac's, the lions, the griffons, the sphinxes, History drawn by six horses galloping atop Rossi's crooked arch, the Nevsky Prospekt, and the Griboyedov Canal. Then he concludes:

> Yet all this beauty was built by Russians—men who ground their teeth and cursed as they rotted in those dismal swamps. The bones of our forefathers were compressed, petrified, fused into palaces coloured ochre, *sang-de-boeuf,* chocolate brown, green.[3]

If those Russians had found an exit, Leningrad today would have been a poorer place. Because they couldn't (or didn't!), they have left for all time a place of incalculable beauty. Solzhenitsyn sees this, but he sees even further again, because he goes on to ask about our disturbed chaotic lives:

> ...What of our explosions of protest, the groans of men shot by firing squads, the tears of our women. .... Can it, too, give rise to such perfect, everlasting beauty?[4]

It is where people are prepared to accept the closed doors, or (in traditional terminology) to take up their cross, that God fulfills his purposes and produces a ray of hope across the darkness—and it is this ray of hope, more than the talking about it, that communicates.

We referred earlier to Jimmy and Alison Porter in John Osborne's play *Look Back in Anger.* Theirs is a marriage that has never really worked. He despises her and everything about her, and she (for love of him) is willing to be a doormat. Jimmy thinks that the only thing that could elicit any sort of feeling from her would be if she were to have a baby and lose it, which is exactly what happens—only not before each of them has tried to exit. Alison goes off because she just can't stand it any longer, and Jimmy has an affair with Alison's friend, Helena. It doesn't work; and when Alison has lost the baby, she comes back. By this time the affair between Jimmy and Helena has also proved itself to be unworkable and Helena has gone. The play ends with the forlorn couple sitting down on the floor and facing each other. They are ready for a new beginning. But yet it is more than a new beginning—it is a fresh start with a new hope. But they can only build a new relationship because they have come face-to-face with the fact that for both of them there is no way out.

Some aspects of this truth may be demonstrated in an extended way by a dramatization (or semi-dramatization) of one of the best and most straightforward human stories found in Ernest Gordon's *Through the Valley of the Kwai,*[5] though I am bound to say some of my congregation managed to miss the point—or perhaps they saw it and reacted against it. We tackled it on Easter Sunday morning as being most appropriate, and we called it "Life in a Morgue."

We started by having the choir sing one verse of "Low in the Grave He Lay," followed by a prayer of invocation and the hymn "This Joyful Eastertide." We then set the scene: first, a letter on tape of a man, Ernest Gordon, dying in a Japanese P.O.W. camp and writing his last letter to his parents. Two readers went on to describe what had happened—how he had been involved in building the bridge over the River Kwai during enormous heat, with long hours of work, and inadequate food until he was nearly dead. We told how, in fact, in that camp death was everywhere, how the Japanese violated every civilized code and had special refinements for prisoners who did not comply with certain orders, how respect for life and property was at its lowest ebb. Then everyone in church responded by singing "Lift Up Your Hearts," except that we began with the second verse ("Above the level of the former years") and sang the first verse as the closing verse of the hymn.

Next, we had a section called "The Hospital and the Gardener." At that time we produced a dramatized reading on tape of two morgue attendants moving our dying man (Gordon) at his own request from the hospital to the morgue because he feels the hospital is so grim that even the morgue couldn't be worse. They tell him to make sure he moves if anyone comes near him; otherwise they might bury him before he's dead.

We followed this tape with another brief description from two readers of how at that moment Gordon was found by a man called Dusty, who cared for him. Dusty was a Methodist. But he was also a gardener, and he had gardener's hands. When he dressed Gordon's wounds, he handled them with the care of a man handling delicate roots. We then crossed the reference with the choir singing "Good Joseph Had a Garden."

At that point we inserted a brief telling of the story of Angus McGillivray, with a Scotsman in the role of storyteller. We did it because if anybody by now was missing the thread, this story told them the whole thing in a nutshell. We did it also because this story effectively epitomizes in one man and one incident what the gospel is all about.

Angus belonged to the Argylls where every man had a mucker— a pal or friend with whom he shared (or mucked-in) everything he had. Angus's mucker was going to die. This was obvious to everyone except Angus. He made up his mind that his mucker would live. Somebody stole his mucker's blankets; so Angus gave him his own. Every mealtime Angus got his ration, but he didn't eat it—he gave it to his mucker, and that was a high price to pay because Angus was a big man who needed food. Then everybody noticed that Angus took to slipping out of the camp at night. His friends thought he was going into the Thai villages to sell black-market goods. They were surprised, because Angus was a man of high principles; but they respected him so much they didn't hold it against him. In the end, as you may guess, the mucker got better— Angus died of starvation! His friends remembered the words from John, "Greater love hath no man than this. . . ."

We sang the hymn "Love's Redeeming Work Is Done" and noted that men in the camp started to talk about Angus's sacrifice. Soon he was not the only one. Here and there men were learning to die for others. The event was the communication.

Part Three we called "The Resurrection." Thanks to the care of the gardener, Ernest Gordon himself began to live, and new life seemed to be running right through the camp. The very place where only months before there had been nothing but despair and indifference to life now became a place where life mattered and hope was born. Ezekiel 37 and Acts 2 were appropriate readings.

So, too, was the Gelineau singing version of Psalm 125 with its refrain, "Those who sow in tears and sorrow will reap with joy." We told of the cobbler and the engineer who teamed up to make artificial legs, of the creation of an orchestra and the making of musical instruments, of the sudden care for the sick, and the reintroduction of a simple funeral service for the dying in the prison camp.

Perhaps the most remarkable result of all was the way in which prisoners who previously could have cut the throats of their oppressors were now able to forgive them. When the war was nearly over, these men who had suffered so much at the hands of the Japanese were being moved by train and were shunted onto a siding where they found themselves beside some dying Japanese soldiers for whom not even the Japanese were caring. Ernest Gordon and his fellow-prisoners got out of the train and started caring for them. An allied officer who witnessed the scene just couldn't believe his eyes. "How can you do this for a people who have inflicted so much suffering on you?" he asked. It was only because the death of one man had enabled others to live without an exit and to accept the closed doors that they had found a fresh door opening to a new future.

There are some people, and Jesus is one of them, who are not only content to live without exits but who also positively close the doors behind them and look only to the future. *Jesus closed the doors* when he set off for Jerusalem, turned out the money changers from the temple, and waited to be arrested. From that moment there was no escape and no compromise. Then it was apparent, as it had never been apparent before, that he was a man of destiny. He put out his hand and clutched the nettle. This is perhaps the greatest sermon he ever preached.

If you want to find such a person in real life, it may be worth, first of all, taking a close look at Celia Coplestone in T. S. Eliot's *The Cocktail Party*. Of course, there is nothing here that you couldn't find by looking at Jesus, but the removal of the halo that surrounds him and the fresh setting may bring out some choice aspects of the experience which otherwise would be missed. Celia is a fictitious character who, after a broken love affair, consults a psychiatrist. He recognizes in her a choice spirit, and he offers her an open door. He can reconcile her to her loss and send her back to life, but there is, he adds, another way,

... unknown, and so requires faith—
The kind of faith that issues from despair.
The destination cannot be described;
You will know very little until you get there;
You will journey blind. But the way leads towards possession
Of what you have sought for in the wrong place.[6]

Celia decides to close the door and journey out into the unknown. Later we learn that she finished up in Kinkanja, as one of three sisters in a nursing order. In that village, the monkeys were very destructive, but they could not be destroyed because the natives believed them to be sacred. However, some of the people who had been converted to Christianity did not accept this belief and killed the monkeys. After this happened, many of the natives were stricken with the plague and blamed the Christians for killing the monkeys. Rebellion broke out, and two of the three sisters escaped—one died in the jungle and the other will never again be fit for normal life. Celia stayed at her post—and all that her rescuers found were just pieces of her body. It would seem that she was crucified near an anthill.

The psychiatrist says that right from the start he recognized her as a woman of destiny—once she decided to close the doors on her former life, then something of this sort was inevitable.

Having seen God incarnate (that is, in flesh) and not only incarnate in Jesus but in humanity, the next step is to go on and find someone in real life. This is inevitably more difficult because in fiction you can create the character just as you want, whereas in real life the character never quite fits.

Even so, when we think of incarnation, identification, and closing doors, I am impressed by the claims of Grace Halsell, a journalist in the United States who decided to take medication in order to turn herself black. She closed the door on a world that was safe and white to discover what it felt like to be a Negro.

She went first to Harlem and found that the medication had caused her feet to swell. A Negro who took pity on her set her in his own car and took her to the hospital. She was examined by a white doctor who immediately implied she shouldn't have dared to come to the hospital with nothing more serious than swollen feet—only a knife in her side, a bullet in her chest, an overdose, or a miscarriage could qualify! He told her it was only blisters. *"You people* should bathe more often—your feet are *dirty!"* he said. Suddenly Grace became aware that she had closed the doors on a world where she was a person. She was now just "one of those people."[7]

She went shopping and discovered why Negroes are not price conscious or quality conscious. They are the victims of fast sales talk. No price tags—one dollar down and the rest to come! They are led on by a contract with such complicated terms that they can't understand it. And even if right were on their side, they feel as if they could never win in a court of law. This time Grace became aware that she had closed the doors on a world where she has rights—now she did not even have the right to complain.

She moved to Mississippi to get the feel of the deep South. Later she sat in a waiting room at the State Employment Agency waiting for her name to be called by a white woman who sat behind a desk. The job she got was that of "daily domestic" for five dollars a day! On arrival at one job, she was not even asked to have a cup of coffee, and it was made plain that she should not use the front door. In another home, her mistress talked to her and unburdened herself of all kinds of confidences, but Grace was not expected to listen and certainly not to answer as an equal. She had closed the doors on a world where she could live—now all she had to do was to hew the wood and draw the water.

We must not misjudge Grace, much less must we reject her, because she became white again. Even traditional theology allows the Son of God to close the doors on heaven and come to earth; but when his suffering was ended and his mission fulfilled, he was allowed to return to heaven. But once you have met a Celia and a Grace, they add a new dimension to life, and it is this aspect that preaches. Since many people are dull of sight and sound, it preaches all the more if you have someone who can deftly focus attention on it.

In this respect there is a delicately self-confessed touch in Malcolm Muggeridge's book *Something Beautiful for God,* the story of Mother Teresa. He begins by saying that he himself lived in Calcutta in the mid-thirties when he was working on the *Statesman,* and he found the place, even with all the comforts of European life (the refrigerator, the servants, etc.), barely tolerable. Moreover, conditions then "were by no means as bad as they are today."

One evening, as Muggeridge was being driven in his car, his driver knocked someone down. Knowing the commotion that would quickly ensue, his driver jumped out, put the man inside, and ran him off to the hospital. Muggeridge insisted on seeing that the man was properly attended to and "was able to follow him into the emergency ward. It was a scene of inconceivable confusion and horror, with patients . . . everywhere." Then they brought in a man who had just cut his throat, and it was more than Muggeridge could stand. He left and hurried back to his apartment for a stiff whisky and soda, to write articles on Bengal's wretched social conditions, what a scandal it was, and how the authorities should . . . etc., etc.

Then came the confession, "I ran away and stayed away; Mother Teresa moved in and stayed."[8] There you have all the difference between natural man and spiritual man, and there you have an insight into the meaning of incarnation. The sermon is not what the incarnate God says, much less what his servants say of him. The sermon is the incarnate God himself, who moves in and stays, closes the doors behind him, and looks only to the future. He it is who releases a new power for men.

Finally, as in previous chapters, what we have seen to be true must not only be true in the message that we preach, but it must also be seen to be true in the life we live and particularly in the life of the church. The church and the preacher that are willing to die must ensure that far from dying of old age they die because they are people of destiny.

So far there has been too much evidence on both sides of the Atlantic that if the church is going to die it will only be from the death of old age. She may resolutely affirm her belief in death and resurrection, and indeed she may celebrate the resurrection on the first day of the week. But suggest to her that perhaps she has to die in the interests of renewal, and as often as not you will be met by a look of blank amazement. With difficulty we can change, but it takes a miracle to bring us to the point of surrender.

The final test for the church is whether she can claim her destiny. Can she go out to where the people are even if this means the death of her internal structures? Can she behave as if it were more important to fight in the field than to preserve her headquarters? Can she put her people in the world even if this means that her own doors may be closed for six days of the week? Can she see her buildings as existing for the masses instead of seeing the masses as existing to keep her buildings in good trim? And instead of trying to get society within herself, can she blow the breath of God through society?

All these are far-reaching questions, both for the minister himself and also for the church, but in working out the answers together, we come face-to-face with our destiny. There will come a point where we meet the Red Sea. Either we give up and return to where we were, or we go on even if we are threatened with drowning in the going. Or, in New Testament terms, either we surrender or we face the cross.

It is not enough that we know what the right answer is. It is only enough if we can do it, for what communicates loudest is what we *do*. Furthermore, only when a man is prepared to face death at first hand for the sake of others does he begin to see why he is living.

There was one evening when a cartoon about a little duck which couldn't swim came on television. His mother and all his brothers and sisters took naturally to the water and didn't even notice that he, the last of the row, was left hovering on the bank. A cat, spying his dilemma, gave chase and so occupied most of the cartoon time, but in the end the little duck came down to the very edge of the water (which ought to have been his trump card) and still did not dare to go in. The cat jumped right over him into the pond and was on the point of drowning. It was this that touched the little duck's heart! Water or no water, the sight of a drowning enemy was too much for him. In he went and performed the rescue. In that very act of sacrifice he learned to swim. The film ended as he swam off with the rest of the family.

Yevtushenko, the Russian poet, tells how as a boy he went on a geological expedition. The thing that frightened him most was that he had never learned to swim, and he was afraid that other members of the team would find out. One day when he and a colleague were walking along a narrow track, the ground gave way under his friend who was in front of him. His friend grabbed at a bush and missed, falling headlong into some water down below and thrashing about in it helplessly because his knapsack was full of pieces of rock samples. Yevtushenko didn't stop even to think. He took off his own knapsack and dived in. He cut the straps of his friend's knapsack and helped him to safety. It was only when it was all over, he wrote afterwards, that he remembered he couldn't swim.[9]

Too often preachers and churches are deprived of this sort of experience because they are unwilling to take the plunge; yet it is only in the acceptance of our death and destiny that we begin to appreciate what Jesus meant when he said, "Whoever seeks to gain his life will lose it, but whoever loses his life will preserve it " (Luke 17:33). (For the same saying with slightly different emphases, see Matthew 10:39; Mark 8:35; John 12:25.)

If we preach the sermon well and the message is clear, there will follow the response that is the natural *end* of a church service or encounter, but the true *beginning* of worship. It may find formal expression in the offertory and in the prayers and in the hymns, but the real response will be in the rest of life. Like Isaiah, we have heard the call, and the appropriate answer is,

"Here am I! Send me" (Isaiah 6:8).

RESPONSE

Response to the presentation of the gospel may be of two kinds. First, there is the unpredictable response that follows from an individual's or a church's willingness to sacrifice and die. This response is not something that any preacher can engineer. He must have sufficient faith in the Good News itself to believe that something he has presented leads to humility and sacrifice, that all this is part of God's plan and therefore each death must lead to renewal. If he tries "to fix it," he will lay himself open to the charge which the early Jews made against the disciples—that they had taken away the body and rigged the story for their own ends. True resurrection is not taking away the body so as to support your story; it is allowing the body to appear when it will and where it will in its own way.

Unfortunately, preachers who have placed much stress on this type of response often feel as if the ground has been cut from under their feet by what we have just said about leaving the matter in God's hands. They may feel this way because not sufficient attention has been paid to the second kind of response. This is the response of the congregation there and then to what has happened. It may not be an act of great moment or world-shattering significance. It may or may not lead to greater faith on the earth. It may or may not lead to anything that other members of the congregation see or hear. But if the proclamation is to be effective, it must lead to something; for the worst possible thing that could happen is that people should go away as if nothing had happened.

This aspect of response is often neglected, possibly because we are too ardently looking for a new experience, a new convert, or a death and resurrection situation.

The nature of the response will vary according to what is presented and the personal lives of the recipients. In some cases it will be a response to a new idea, either to accept it or reject it. This kind of response may be dismissed by some as education rather than worship, but it is a false distinction. It can be just as worshipful to embrace (or reject) a fresh idea as it can be to give expression to some fresh emotion. We are minds as well as feelings. In other cases, however, there will be an emotional response, which again needs to be specific, not just a vague feeling of warmth or satisfaction, but more the kind of pulsating emotion that we associate with the end of a baseball game—sometimes thrill, sometimes anger, sometimes disappointment, sometimes frustration. Far better to have any or all of these emotions after an act of worship than to leave the place just looking bored. In still other cases, it will be a response of the will. The worshiper will know that he must go out and do something. These are the responses that a preacher has a right to work for and to look for, because he knows that if he can achieve these kinds of things, his presentation of the gospel will lead to the fuller and richer response with which we started this chapter.

Our mistake, however, has been not so much that we have failed to achieve response in our worship as that we have failed to give people an opportunity to give expression to their response. In a few churches in Britain, though perhaps more generally in the United States, the preacher gives an opportunity to any who wish to register a definite commitment to Jesus Christ or perhaps make an inquiry about his way of life. But apart from that, any response has been muted. A warm feeling of joy may be expressed in the singing of a hymn, but sharing a new idea or exploring it is ruled out because all talking is discouraged. If a person wants to express a new sense of belonging to the fellowship by shaking hands with his neighbor before the service ends, the gesture would be regarded by many with suspicion.

A theological teacher once said in a lecture on teaching method that he encourages a student, when he has been reading a book for a certain length of time, to make some practical response to it. He may hug it, kiss it, throw it across the room, or stamp on it, but it is most important that he should make some response. If he does not, then the pent-up reaction will only break out somewhere else. The student may still have to go on reading the book even if he hates it, but at least now he knows how he stands in relation to it.

The preacher has sometimes experienced this reaction in the form of the worshiper who storms out of church protesting about the drafts or the heating in the building, which is probably no different from what it has been on other Sundays. But something has disturbed him, and he might have gone away from church a healthier being if only he had been able to give expression to the actual cause of his reaction.

In some churches the practice of placing the sermon earlier in the service and following it by the offering (itself one kind of expression) and the main prayers of thanksgiving and intercession has much to commend it. But to be really effective, the opportunity to react needs to be thrown open to the congregation. Just how it is done depends on the size of the congregation and the nature of the building. In some Russian Baptist churches members of the congregation write down their topics for prayer on pieces of paper and pass them to the front, and so the prayers of the church really are offered on the altar. In some cases I have simply suggested broad areas of concern and invited members of the congregation to fill in the details in silence. At other times I have simply asked the congregation, in the light of the theme of the worship and sermon, whom (or what) they felt we should give thanks for and whom they felt we should remember in our prayers. Once people get used to hearing their voices in church, the habit can be helpful to everybody. Not only do they have a chance to make their response and allow the prayers of the church to be the prayers of the church, but their responses may also introduce a whole new set of ideas and concepts which the leader of worship has not even seen. Moreover, if congregational response is combined with the earlier suggestion of getting people committed to a point of view earlier in the service, it is rewarding occasionally to have a member praying for someone who forty minutes before meant little or nothing to him. That this experience happens in many worshipers who remain silent need not be doubted. The response is there.

This procedure is a start, but the preacher should be aware that if he begins here, he may be opening a floodgate. Once a congregation finds its voice, there are sure to be some present who will not be content simply to make a few suggestions for prayer. They may well wish to examine the roots of faith or practice, even if not actually to lay the axe to them.

A second useful step therefore is to shorten the first part of the worship and reduce the sermon (on occasions) to little more than "a starter" or a short discourse that presents a one-sided point of view. Then the preacher may come and sit at the level of his congregation, answer their questions, or engage in discussion with them. This enables those who wish to respond with their minds to do so, though care must also be taken to provide some adequate response for those who feel more than they think. The practical element also must not be lost sight of for the sake of those who want to do something. Moreover, if it is felt that the new method is detracting from the traditional emphasis, the balance may be restored by keeping the subject matter on traditional lines. We tried several services after this fashion, for example, with puzzling parables.

Another possibility is to give people the opportunity of responding to a person rather than to anything that is actually said or done, and this is where the carefully conducted interview can occasionally replace the sermon with some profit. There are two reasons for this. One is that most people will respond more readily to a person than they will to anything that is said. The other reason is that if you want your congregation to meet a person, it is much better to introduce the person and his story in a skillful fashion to the congregation than simply to let him stand up and talk. The preacher knows his congregation. He must also know the guest and his story. The preacher's task is to allow the one to speak to the other in such a way as to elicit a response.

To achieve this result, the preacher who attempts the interview must know very clearly what he is about, for the biggest single factor is that the congregation respond to the person as a person. Once the method is established, people may be interviewed who will provoke a negative reaction, but to begin with discretion may be the better part of valor. Moreover, it is best to avoid using the interview when you simply want to elicit information or, for that matter, when you want to assess a man's ideas or point of view, perhaps by examining his latest book. In the first case, a straight talk is probably best, and in the second, a wider than a one-to-one discussion could be more helpful. But when you know of someone who has had a worthwhile experience and a good story to tell, which can lead the congregation either to thankfulness or concern, that person is worth talking to. Ply him with questions, in which you not only learn what happened, but also how, why, and (most important) what the experience meant to him and to others.

By this point, members of the congregation are likely to have been made so aware of the inroads that have been made into the traditional patterns of worship that they will begin to ask questions about the rest. Once questions are asked, it soon becomes apparent that though the plan of preparation, word, and response provides a good framework, things don't actually happen just like that in real life. Some worshipers make their responses early in the service. Others hear the word during the last hymn. Therefore, once we know what the theological and liturgical patterns are, and once we have practiced them enough to be aware of them, we do not need always to confine the response to the end or the confession to the beginning. The door is open for a wider and a more flexible handling of the whole act of worship. Moreover, a congregation which has begun by making suggestions for prayers and then has proceeded to have a crack at the sermon is not going to be content unless it can run its own services. And why not? Worship is meant to be an act of the whole congregation. At times (and in the nature of the case it is not likely to be very often) there is no reason why the preacher should not be more like the conductor of an orchestra than a solo performer. When he tries, he will soon discover whether he actually knows how to conduct worship or whether all he can do is to wave a baton.

One way of achieving this larger participation is by inviting a group of members to prepare the worship for a given service. But unless more spadework is done, the likelihood is that they will simply choose hymns and readings and invite one of their number to speak. Several months of preparation are needed, therefore, in which the preacher makes clear that the act of proclamation is the whole service. In saying that, I am not simply saying that the hymns, readings, and prayers must be related to the sermon. I am saying that the whole thing should be planned as a unit from start to finish, rather like writing a play, and that the preacher should cultivate the habit of using hymns, readings, songs, music, even tapes and visual aids, in whatever order or pattern most effectively tells the story and elicits a response.

The simplest way of achieving this effect is by signposting. Where there is a printed order of service, the congregation should not need to be told the number of the hymn or the reference for the reading. But it does need to be told, in a sentence, what is the point of the particular selection, how it relates to what has just gone before or what is to follow. If a preacher cannot explain how the selection helps the flow and gives unity, then he should look closely at the item in question and see whether it has any right to be there. If the pattern and the purpose are clear, then it becomes easier to substitute songs for hymns, nonbiblical readings for biblical lessons, and visual aids for traditional prayer without members feeling that the structure has cracked. They will be able to follow the service even if some items are unfamiliar.

Once members of the congregation realize the basic pattern, they are slowly being delivered from the traditional type of worship. They begin to see the wood rather than the trees, and form becomes less important than content. At this stage a few members, under the leadership of the minister, may begin to plan an act of worship together. We tried this in two ways.

In the first case we invited each of our Bible and Life (House) Study Groups to prepare an act of worship on its theme for the winter, which happened to be freedom. One group simply took the traditional pattern of worship, collected a lot of material on the theme as they saw it, filled the appropriate slots, and supplied me with the raw material for the sermon. Another group took over the whole hour and presented different aspects of the subject using different groups of readers.

A second attempt at group preparation sprang from our concern about Peter L. Berger's *A Rumor of Angels,* to which we referred in chapter 2. In that case a handpicked group of four worked for a whole winter with me and produced four services on different aspects, most of which bore little relation to the familiar pattern of worship and yet which presented some aspect of Christian truth and which looked for response.

In both cases the difficulties of group presentation arose from the difficulty of developing a complete service to span a period of 45-50 minutes. So we next selected a theme as a basis for worship and invited groups or individuals in the church to supply a single item or interpretation of the theme lasting not more than four minutes. Subjects chosen were fairly general: hunger, wealth, waste, censorship, and leisure. In every case, I undertook to supply one major part of the service, either a film, a discussion, or a review, plus a brief five-minute exposition closely approximating a sermonette to insure that there was some overt theological content or comment. The sections did not always necessarily relate very closely to one another, but the word was heard and a response elicited, sometimes here, sometimes there, and sometimes even in the juxtaposition of two pieces.

A more useful pattern of worship, especially in the early stages of experiment and transformation, came to be known as the integrated day. Possibly this approach is more directly appropriate to the British situation where it is still fairly general to have two services every Sunday even though most members will attend only one. It is a very simple device whereby instead of taking two different *themes* for two services that are more or less alike in pattern (morning and evening), one theme is chosen for two different kinds of *service* on the same day. This approach is also a most useful device for weaning people away from the traditional order of service. We take a theme for the day, and in the morning we explore it in the context of our normal service. Then in the evening we scrap everything and start from scratch. Taking the same theme, we will use any device at hand which will enable people to appreciate and enter into the theme, sharing in confession, thanksgiving, intercession, or whatever seems appropriate. Worshipers attending both services have the advantage of seeing a theme of worship from more than one angle. Those who attend only one service have the choice of taking it straight or taking it different.

Almost any theme is fair game, but to strike home, the worship needs to be anchored at two points. It needs to be anchored first in the congregation, arising out of the congregation's experience and involvement in society. At the same time it needs to be anchored in the community by involving the members of the community who will not normally be found in the church's worship.

Within our church community, for example, we have a small group of people interested in mental health. We had a club for mentally handicapped children meeting on the premises with a number of our members as helpers, and we had a social worker in the membership with good local community contacts. A day's worship on mental health seemed a good idea. For the morning service there was no shortage of good biblical material. What did Jesus actually do, and with what results? In the evening we made a point of inviting local workers, societies, and clubs to share the event with us. We also invited parents and friends of mentally handicapped people who were known to us. We showed them a film on the stress and strain of caring for a mentally handicapped child, and then I conducted a discussion about the film, using a social worker, a psychiatrist, and a parent. Were I doing the same thing now, I would certainly involve the congregation more in the discussion as a whole.

On another occasion we had a similar day devoted to the theme of police, probation, and after-care, chiefly because another group of members were involved in this field as magistrate, probation officer, and volunteer prison visitor. They were asked to share their experiences and concern with their fellow-members. It was a good opportunity also for them to invite their friends and colleagues and to build a bridge between church and community. In the evening they presented the case of Adrian Smith, a fictitious character who had been brought before the court for some relatively minor offense. They asked the congregation to pass judgment. Should Adrian Smith be fined, put on probation, or sent to prison? A small panel consisting of the prison visitor, a magistrate, and a probation officer then assessed each method of punishment in turn, showing the strengths and weaknesses of each and engaging in a discussion with members of the congregation as they did so. At the very least, the service was a piece of public relations or Christian education, but it had within it the seeds of that sort of worship where the eyes of the blind are opened and the man who has been deaf for years suddenly begins to hear.

The presence of children in an act of worship and their ability to share in what is happening can have a relaxing effect on others, provided the children are not used simply as stooges to entertain the adults or to get the point across. Indeed it is probably better to address the congregation as a whole and allow the children to steal the stage if they wish than to try directly to appeal to the children as such.

In a series of services, especially planned with young people in mind, on the theme "Exploring Our Senses," the children very quickly found their own niche as one week we explored God's gift of sight and another we listened to sounds and identified them. But when we came to explore our sense of touch, they came into their own. Three or four of the youngest were given an opportunity to choose something that they liked to handle out of a dozen different kinds of material. Many members of the congregation can still remember one little girl standing there on the rostrum just enjoying the feel of a piece of sheepskin, first on her hands, then on her face, then on her neck. Others remember the little boy who picked up a hammerhead, a wire brush, and a piece of sandpaper; he loved them because they were rough. The children aptly illustrated the way in which we are different, but most of all they showed to everybody what it was to worship with a touch.

In that situation the response just can't be tied down to any particular moment in the liturgy, though it may find expression at some focal point. The response is there as it happens. Worshipers go home feeling that something has happened; and when that is the case, God has his opportunity.

But even so there is another aspect to response that must not be overlooked. Not only must we give people a variety of events to which they can respond, but also at times they must be allowed to respond to a quite different kind of situation.

Two years ago, when I was discussing the forthcoming pattern of summer services with my church officers, one of them said, "Why do we never worship anywhere but in church? Why can't we get out-of-doors?" The thought of an old-fashioned type of open-air meeting with passersby there to gape was not exactly what I was looking for, but suddenly I remembered that when I was on tour in the United States in 1967, I preached one July Sunday morning at First Baptist Church, Providence, Rhode Island, and in the afternoon the whole church made a trip to the little chapel in the open air down by the sea. After a picnic, on a warm and sunny evening we all sat out-of-doors for an evening service. Could we achieve that atmosphere in Britain?

Eight miles from our town of Worthing is Arundel Castle, set in beautiful grounds and owned by the Duke of Norfolk, a Roman Catholic. What were the chances that he would allow us the use of a corner of the grounds, with quietness and privacy, for a picnic and an act of worship? A local Baptist in Arundel knew how to ask and that was that. It would be an occasion to unite with our brethren in Arundel—and on Roman Catholic territory, too.

The first year there was a drenching rain, and after an hour steeling ourselves to enjoy the moments out-of-doors between the showers, we all took refuge in the church hall belonging to the local Baptists and we had our picnic. But we followed it with a short act of worship and breaking of bread, and the whole service came over in a fresh way. We belonged to one another in a way that we did not belong when we sat in our formal rows in church. The following year the day was incredibly hot. We played and we ate together, and we had a new awareness of ourselves as a family. Worship, though brief, again took on new meaning in a new setting, but most important of all was the fact that the variation in setting meant that nobody could be bored or indifferent. Everybody made some response.

I believe the idea needs further development. We are all familiar with some of the benefits that come from worshiping in a church of a different tradition, but how often do we try worshiping in an unfamiliar setting and then allowing the setting to dictate our worship?

Gifford House, for example, in Worthing is a home for the wounded and disabled of two world wars. You can't go there without being aware of 1914–1918 and 1939–1946. Every November in Britain, churches mark Remembrance Sunday by remembering the dead of two world wars. There is usually a period of silence, special prayers, and there may or may not be an appropriate sermon. But the service is always somewhat remote from current experience. What would happen if a congregation were to move into Gifford House on Remembrance Sunday for a sandwich meal and a couple of hours? Let one member brief the congregation on the nature of the House and what goes on there. Then have a free time for people to talk to staff and residents, to look at pictures, and to read plaques. Finally, invite them to come together for twenty minutes and see what acts of confession or thanksgiving are appropriate. Read the Scriptures, sing a hymn, and conduct a meditation. I haven't tried this approach, but I have no doubt that if it were done, Remembrance Sunday would come alive in a new way. A visit to a Veterans' Hospital in the United States on a Sunday preceding Memorial Day or Veterans' Day would lead to much the same kind of experience.

A little farther along the road is Ford Prison, an open prison where there are "con" men, embezzlers, and men of high professional standing who have been guilty of fraudulent conversion. I don't suppose the authorities would ever agree, but one Sunday I would like to take my congregation there. Worship would have a different feel about it. The congregation would find it impossible to accept the same old platitudes, and the preacher would find it impossible to utter them. Of course, I don't rule out that our presence might have some value for the residents, but my main concern would be to put my congregation in a situation where God can speak in a new way and they can make a fresh response.

A little farther to the north of Arundel there is St. Julian's at Coolham, a Christian community with an atmosphere all its own. Possibly a whole weekend here would be needed to capture the atmosphere. What an experience there could be if we could express our worship in terms of our normal life and tradition, but changed and transformed by the place where the worship was held!

Different places would offer different interests. In an industrial area a church ought to choose a factory, preferably at a time of economic and industrial unrest. In a university town the university itself may offer a relatively easy starting place. Usually there is a hospital, a school, some law courts, and possibly a race course or a golf course or the scene of some other sporting event where worship could be held.

It would not be new for the church to worship in a strange place. We have often done this. What would be new would be that the preacher and the congregation should soak themselves in their new environment and then, in a shared experience, allow their worship to arise out of it. Others who lived there or who had been sharing in the same experience, for example, at a sporting event, could then easily be invited to share in the experience. In this way public worship would again become the worship of God in public. Worshiping in this fashion would also add a new dimension to life and allow worship to become a living experience.

In large churches particularly, all of the congregation might not be able to go. There might not be sufficient accommodations for them. But would this matter? Such worship wouldn't be happening every week. In some cases the whole congregation might visit the same place over a period of three months, with eight or ten people going on each occasion. In other cases the whole congregation might go out at once, but to different places. It would not matter, and in many cases the smaller group might be more beneficial. Margaret Potts quotes an American Christian worker who organized discussion groups in Greenwich Village, New York, as saying, "I had to ration the number of Christians in my group because if I didn't, the discussion became so unreal as to be valueless." [1] Such occasions would also be of immense value in that children and young people could enter into the experience from a very early age and gain something from them.

As of now I suspect this is the next section of the road we need to tread together. All that we have said and done so far will prove to have been a preparation for it, for it will have taught a congregation what to look for and how to interpret it. Only when we have taken this step will we begin to see where we should turn next. But each experience in turn will be its own preaching occasion. For as the Word takes flesh, something happens in the heart of man to bring conviction.

It is not likely, I think, that the practice will be carried to excess or that the worship "away from home" will take over. But should we be worried if it did? After all, the early Christians were certainly not addicted to their buildings; and if we found ourselves engaging steadily in patterns of worship on the hills, by the sea, in the city centers, and in the places where men live, work, and play, drawing our illustrations as well as our themes from the things that were around us and coping with each situation as it arrived—why, then indeed, we might be forgiven for thinking we were right back in the New Testament situation and in the Gospels with Jesus.

Such an experience would indeed be a preaching situation, and something would surely happen!

BOOK LIST

Albee, Edward, *The Zoo Story*. Harmondsworth: Penguin Books Ltd., 1962; New York: Coward, McCann & Geoghegan, Inc., 1960.

Anderson, David, *The Tragic Protest: A Christian Study of Some Modern Literature*. London: S.C.M. Press Ltd., 1969; Richmond: John Knox Press, 1970.

Ashley, Jack, *Journey into Silence*. London: Bodley Head Ltd., 1973.

Baxter, Kay, *Speak What We Feel*. London: S.C.M. Press Ltd., 1964.

Beason, Trevor, *An Eye for an Ear*. London: S.C.M. Press Ltd., 1972.

Berger, Peter L., *A Rumor of Angels*. Harmondsworth: Pelican Books, 1948; Garden City, New York: Doubleday & Company, Inc., 1969.

Campling, Christopher, and Davis, Michael, *Words for Worship*. London: Edward Arnold Ltd., 1969.

Camus, Albert, *The Plague*. Harmondsworth: Penguin Books Ltd., 1948; New York: Alfred A. Knopf, Inc., 1964.

Cox, Harvey G., *On Not Leaving It to the Snake*. London: S.C.M. Press Ltd., 1968; New York: The Macmillan Company, 1964.

Cox, Harvey G., *The Secular City.* London: S.C.M. Press Ltd., 1965; New York: The Macmillan Company, 1965.

de Jesus, Carolina Maria, *Beyond All Pity.* London: Panther Books Ltd., 1962. See also *Child of the Dark: The Diary of Carolina Maria de Jesus,* trans. by David St. Clair. New York: E.P. Dutton and Co., Inc., 1962.

de Saint-Exupéry, Antoine, *The Little Prince.* London: Heinemann Educational Books Ltd., n.d.; New York: Harcourt Brace Jovanovich, Inc., 1973.

Dodd, C. H., *Apostolic Preaching and Its Developments.* London: Hodder and Stoughton Ltd., 1936; New York: Harper & Row, Publishers, 1939.

Dunkerly, R., *Beyond the Gospels.* Harmondsworth: Penguin Books Ltd., 1957.

Eliot, T. S., *The Cocktail Party.* London: Faber & Faber Ltd., 1940; *The Complete Poems and Plays 1909-1950.* New York: Harcourt Brace Jovanovich, Inc., 1952.

Evans, J. J., *Guard Our Unbelief.* London: Oxford University Press, 1971.

Gordon, Ernest, *Through the Valley of the Kwai.* New York: Harper & Row, Publishers, 1962; *Miracle on the River Kwai.* London: Fontana Books, 1963.

Gray, Martin, and Gallo, Max, *For Those I Loved.* London: Bodley Head Ltd., 1973; Boston: Little, Brown & Company, 1972.

Habel, Norman C., *Interrobang.* London: Lutterworth Press, 1969; Philadelphia: Fortress Press, 1969.

Halsell, Grace, *Soul Sister.* London: William Collins Sons & Co., Ltd., n.d.; New York: World Publishing Company, 1969.

Hobden, Sheila M., *Explorations in Worship.* London: Lutterworth Press, 1970.

McLuhan, Marshall, *The Medium Is the Massage.* Harmondsworth: Penguin Books Ltd., 1967; New York: Bantam Books, Inc., 1973.

McLuhan, Marshall, *Understanding Media: The Extensions of Man*. London: Sphere Books Ltd., 1964; New York: Signet, imprint of New American Library, Inc., 1964.

Muggeridge, Malcolm, *Something Beautiful for God*. London: Fontana Books, 1971; New York: Harper & Row, Publishers, 1971.

Osborne, John, *Look Back in Anger*. London: Faber & Faber Ltd., 1957; New York: S. G. Phillips, Inc., 1957.

Potts, Margaret I., *St. Julian's*. London: S.C.M. Press Ltd., 1968.

Quoist, Michel, *Prayers*. Dublin: Gill and Macmillan, 1963; New York: Sheed & Ward, Inc., 1963.

Sharkey, Bernarda, *Growing to Wonder*. Paramus, N.J.: Paulist Press, imprint of Paulist/Newman Press, 1971.

Solzhenitsyn, Alexander, *One Day in the Life of Ivan Denisovich*. London: Sphere Books Ltd., 1970; New York: Ballantine Books, Inc., 1971.

Solzhenitsyn, Alexander, *Stories and Prose Poems*. London: Bodley Head Ltd., 1970; New York: Farrar, Straus & Giroux, Inc., 1971.

Stearn, G. E., ed., *McLuhan Hot and Cool*. Harmondsworth: Penguin Books Ltd., 1968; New York: The Dial Press, 1967.

Stewart, Douglas, *The Ark of God*. London: Carey Kingsgate Press, 1961; Folcroft, Pa.: Folcroft Library Editions, 1973.

Van Buren, Paul, *The Secular Meaning of the Gospel*. London: S.C.M. Press Ltd., 1963; New York: The Macmillan Company, 1963.

Williams, Tennessee, *The Glass Menagerie*. Harmondsworth: Penguin Books Ltd., 1945; New York: New Directions Publishing Corporation, 1949.

Wilson, Dorothy Clarke, *Hilary*. London: Hodder and Stoughton Ltd., 1972; New York: McGraw-Hill Book Company, 1973.

Wölfel, Ursula, *The Light and the Dark*. London: Lutterworth Press, 1972.

Wren-Lewis, John, *What Shall We Tell the Children?* London: Constable & Co. Ltd., 1971.

Yevtushenko, Yevgeny, *A Precocious Autobiography.* Harmondsworth: Penguin Books Ltd., 1963; New York: E.P. Dutton & Co., Inc., 1963.

NOTES

Preface

[1] John G. Davies, *Every Day God* (Naperville, Ill.: Alec R. Allenson, Inc., 1973).
[2] Michael H. Taylor, *Variations on a Theme* (London: Gallaird, 1973).

Introduction

[1] Trevor Beason, *An Eye for an Ear* (London: S.C.M. Press, 1972), p. 11.

[2] Marshall McLuhan, *Understanding Media: The Extensions of Man* (New York: Signet Books, imprint of New American Library, Inc., 1964), pp. 268-294.

[3] *Ibid.*, p. 278.

[4] *Ibid.*, p. 286.

[5] C. H. Dodd, *The Apostolic Preaching and Its Developments* (New York: Willett, Clark & Company, 1937), p. 1.

[6] *Ibid.*, p. 2.

[7] *Ibid.*, p. 3.

[8] *Ibid.*, p. 11.

[9] *Ibid.*, p. 18.

[10] *Ibid.*, p. 28.

Chapter 1

[1] John Wren-Lewis, *What Shall We Tell the Children?* (London: Constable & Company Ltd., 1971), pp. 158-165.

[2] Albert Camus, *The Plague,* translated by Stuart Gilbert (New York: Alfred A. Knopf, Inc., 1964), p. 231.

[3] Edward Albee, *The Zoo Story* (New York: Coward, McCann & Geoghegan, Inc., 1960).

[4] Alexander Solzhenitsyn, "The Bonfire and the Ants," *Stories and Prose Poems*, trans. Michael Glenny (New York: Farrar, Straus & Giroux, Inc., 1971), p. 260. Published in England by The Bodley Head. Reprinted with permission of Farrar, Straus & Giroux, Inc. Translation copyright © 1970, 1971 by Michael Glenny.

[5] Norman C. Habel, *Interrobang* (Philadelphia: Fortress Press, 1969), p. 95.

[6] Christopher Campling and Michael Davis, compilers, *Words for Worship* (London: Edward Arnold [Publishers], Ltd., 1969), #701.

Chapter 2

[1] Ursula Wölfel, *The Light and the Dark* (London: Lutterworth Press, 1972), pp. 33-34.

[2] Douglas Stewart, *The Ark of God* (London: Carey-Kingsgate, 1961); Kay Baxter, *Speak What We Feel* (London: S.C.M. Press, 1964); and J. J. Evans, *Guard Our Unbelief* (London: Oxford University Press, 1971).

[3] John Osborne, *Look Back in Anger* (New York: S. G. Phillips, Inc., 1957).

[4] Peter L. Berger, *A Rumor of Angels* (New York: Doubleday & Company, Inc., 1969), pp. 65-94.

[5] *The Little Prince* is by Antoine de Saint-Exupéry, and it is published in the United States by Harcourt Brace Jovanovich, Inc., and in Britain by Heinemann. The extract used here was taken from Sheila Hobden, *Explorations in Worship* (London: Lutterworth Press, 1970), pp. 81-83. A similar extract from the same book can be found in Bernarda Sharkey, *Growing to Wonder* (Paramus, N.J.: Paulist Press, 1971), pp. 6-7.

[6] Michel Quoist, *Prayers*, trans. Agnes M. Forsyth and Anne Marie de Commaille (New York: Sheed & Ward, Inc., 1963), pp. 3-5.

[7] Martin Gray and Max Gallo, *For Those I Loved,* trans. Anthony White (Boston: Little, Brown and Company, 1972).

Chapter 3

[1] Carolina Maria de Jesus, *Beyond All Pity* (London: Panther, 1962), p. 42. From the book *Child of the Dark: The Diary of Carolina Maria de Jesus*. Trans. David St. Clair. Copyright © 1962 by E. P. Dutton & Co., Inc., and Souvenir Press, Ltd., publishers, and used with their permission.

[2] *Ibid.*, p. 11.

[3] Tennessee Williams, *The Glass Menagerie* (New York: New Directions Books, New Directions Publishing Company, 1949).

[4] Harvey G. Cox, *On Not Leaving It to the Snake* (New York: The Macmillan Company, 1964), p. xiv.

[5] Harvey G. Cox, *The Secular City* (New York: The Macmillan Company, 1965), p. 112.

[6] David Anderson, *The Tragic Protest* (Atlanta: John Knox Press, 1970), p. 94.

[7] Dorothy Clarke Wilson, *Hilary* (New York: McGraw-Hill Book Company, 1972).

Chapter 4

[1] Quoted in R. Dunkerley, *Beyond the Gospels* (Harmondsworth: Penguin Books Ltd., 1957).

[2] Alexander Solzhenitsyn, *One Day in the Life of Ivan Denisovich* (New York: Ballantine Books, Inc., 1971).

[3] Alexander Solzhenitsyn, "The City on the Neva," *Stories and Prose Poems* (New York: Farrar, Straus & Giroux, Inc., 1971), p. 252.

[4] *Ibid.*, pp. 252-253.

[5] Ernest Gordon, *Through the Valley of the Kwai* (New York: Harper & Row, Publishers, 1962).

[6] T. S. Eliot, "The Cocktail Party," *The Complete Poems and Plays 1909–1950* (New York: Harcourt Brace Jovanovich, Inc., 1952), pp. 364-365.

[7] Grace Halsell, *Soul Sister* (New York: World Publishing Company, 1969).

[8] Malcolm Muggeridge, *Something Beautiful for God* (New York: Harper & Row, Publishers, 1971), pp. 21-22.

[9] Yevgeny Yevtushenko, *A Precocious Autobiography*, trans. Andrew R. MacAndrew (New York: E. P. Dutton & Co., Inc., 1963), pp. 45-46.

Chapter 5

[1] Margaret I. Potts, *St. Julian's* (London: S.C.M. Press, 1968), p. 37.